DESERT JOURNEY

Studies in Numbers and Deuteronomy

R. E. HARLOW

EVERYDAY PUBLICATIONS
TORONTO, CANADA   M4C 3T4

PLEASE READ THIS

The Bible is the Word of God and so is the Lord Jesus Christ. The Lord Jesus is both God and Man and the Bible also was given by God through men. The Bible is like a body because every part is important to all the rest. You cannot understand any book in the Bible unless you know something about all the books of the Bible.

Numbers and Deuteronomy are important parts of the Word of God. If you know Numbers and Deuteronomy you will be able to understand better many other parts of the Bible. You will also know more about God, the only true God.

Every day you should read a few verses from the Bible. Read also the part of this book which explains the verses which you have studied. On pages 3 and 4 you will see which verses to read each day. For example on the first day of the first month read Numbers chapter 1, verses 1 to 19 (Numbers 1.1-19. On page 7 you will see a little number on the left side. The number 1/1 means that you start here on the first day of the first month. On page 8, the number 1/2 shows what you should read on the second day.

This plan will help you to read through Numbers and Deuteronomy and these studies in six months. You can start any month. Write in the name of the month at the top of page 3 and the next five months also on pages 3 and 4. If you want to start before the first day of the month read a little every day, then start over again on the first day of the month. If the month has already started you can read every day the verses for two days until you catch up.

Copyright © 1974
by R. E. Harlow

ISBN 0-919586-02-3

Printed in Canada

READ THE BIBLE EVERY DAY

Day	First Month	Second Month	Third Month
1	NUM 1. 1–19	11.16–23	23.13–30
2	1.20–31	11.24–34	24. 1– 9
3	1.32–43	12. 1– 8	24.10–25
4	1.44–54	12. 9–16	25. 1–18
5	2. 1–16	13. 1–16	26. 1–22
6	2.17–34	13.17–29	26.23–51
7	3. 1–13	13.30–33	26.52–65
8	3.14–26	14. 1–10	27. 1–11
9	3.27–38	14.11–25	27.12–23
10	3.39–51	14.26–45	28. 1–15
11	4. 1–16	15. 1–16	28.16–31
12	4.17–33	15.17–31	29. 1–11
13	4.34–49	15.32–41	29.12–25
14	5. 1–10	16. 1–11	29.26–40
15	5.11–31	16.12–24	30. 1–12
16	6. 1–12	16.25–40	30.13–16
17	6.13–27	16.41–50	31. 1– 8
18	7. 1–11	17. 1–13	31. 9–24
19	7.12–35	18. 1–19	31.25–47
20	7.36–59	18.20–32	31.48–54
21	7.60–83	19. 1–10	32. 1–15
22	7.84–89	19.11–22	32.16–27
23	8. 1–19	20. 1–13	32.28–40
24	8.20–26	20.14–29	33. 1–15
25	9. 1–14	21. 1– 9	33.16–40
26	9.15–23	21.10–20	33.41–47
27	10. 1–10	21.21–35	33.48–56
28	10.11–28	22. 1–21	34. 1–15
29	10.29–36	22.22–41	34.16–29
30	11. 1–15	23. 1–12	35. 1– 8

READ THE BIBLE EVERY DAY

Day	Fourth Month	Fifth Month	Sixth Month
1	35. 9–21	7.12–16	24.14–22
2	35.22–29	8. 1–10	25. 1–19
3	35.30–34	8.11–20	26. 1–19
4	36. 1–13	9. 1–12	27. 1–10
5	Frames 1 – 8	9.13–29	27.11–26
6	" 9 – 16	10. 1–11	28. 1–14
7	" 17 – 24	10.12–22	28.15–37
8	" 25 – 32	11. 1–21	28.38–57
9	" 33 – 40	11.22–32	28.58–68
10	" 41 – 47	12. 1–14	29. 1– 9
11	DEUT 1. 1– 5	12.15–32	29.10–29
12	1. 6–18	13. 1–18	30. 1–20
13	1.19–40	14. 1–21	31. 1–13
14	1.41–46	14.22–29	31.14–30
15	2. 1–15	15. 1–11	32. 1–14
16	2.16–23	15.12–23	32.15–36
17	2.24–37	16. 1–12	32.37–43
18	3. 1– 7	16.13–22	32.44–52
19	3. 8–20	17. 1–20	33. 1– 5
20	3.21–29	18. 1–14	33. 6–11
21	4. 1–14	18.15–22	33.12–17
22	4.15–24	19. 1–21	33.18–23
23	4.25–40	20. 1–20	33.24–29
24	4.41–49	21. 1–14	34. 1–12
25	5. 1–15	21.15–23	Frames 1 – 3
26	5.16–27	22. 1–12	" 4 – 6
27	5.28–33	22.13–30	" 7 – 9
28	6. 1–15	23. 1–14	" 10 – 12
29	6.16–25	23.15–25	" 13 – 15
30	7. 1–11	24. 1–13	" 16 – 19

Numbers

Page

1 **At Sinai — Chapters 1 - 6**   7
    The people of Israel were counted for the
    first time, Chapter 1
    Order for the camp and for the journey, Chapter 2
    The Levites, Chapter 3
    Instructions for moving the Tabernacle, Chapter 4
    God commanded the people to be holy, Chapter 5
    Nazirites, Chapter 6

2 **Sinai to Kadesh — Chapters 7 - 12**   20
    The priests began to use the Tabernacle, Chapters 7, 8
    The journey to Kadesh, chapters 9 - 12
    The second Passover, 9.1-14
    The cloud, 9.15-23
    The silver trumpets, 10.1-10
    The first part of the journey, 10.11-36
    The people of Israel complained against God,
       Chapter 11
    Aaron and Miriam were jealous of Moses,
       Chapter 12

3 **Israel rebelled at Kadesh-barnea — Chapters 13-19**   32
    Moses sent men to explore the land, Chapter 13
    The people of Israel rebelled against God, Chapter 14
    Rules for those who would enter the land, Chapter 15
    Korah rebelled against God, Chapter 16
    Aaron's stick sprouted leaves and flowers, Chapter 17
    The portion of the Levites, Chapter 18
    Water for religious purification, Chapter 19

4 **Kadesh to Canaan — Chapters 20 - 25**   46
    Back at Kadesh, Chapter 20
    Journeys and war, Chapter 21
    Balak called Balaam, Chapter 22
    Balaam's first prophecy, 23.1-12
    Balaam's second prophecy, 23.13-25
    Balaam's third prophecy, 23.26 - 24.9

Page

Balaam's fourth prophecy, 24.10-25
Balaam's success, Chapter 25

5 **Commands for Israel in the land of Canaan** 56
    — Chapters 26 - 36
    The people of Israel were counted a second time, Chapter 26
    Women can own property, 27.1-11
    Joshua is appointed to take Moses' place, 27.12-23
    Sacrifices to be offered at certain times of the year, Chapters 28, 29
    Vows of women, Chapter 30
    The Midianites are punished, 31.1-20
    Things taken from the enemy after the battle, 31.21-54
    The request of Reuben and Gad, Chapter 32
    Journeys from Egypt to Jordan, Chapter 33
    Borders of the land of Canaan, Chapter 34
    Cities of refuge, Chapter 35
    More about the daughters of Zelophehad, Chapter 36

6 **What does the book of Numbers teach us?** 67

AT SINAI   1

Numbers is the fourth book of the Bible. It comes after Exodus and Leviticus and before Deuteronomy and Joshua.

In Exodus the Lord told Israel to keep the feast of the Passover, then He led them out of Egypt. At Mount Sinai God gave them His law, and told them to build the Tabernacle, the Tent of God. In Leviticus God gave His people many more laws and rules while they were at Mount Sinai.

In Numbers 1-9 the people of Israel were still at Mount Sinai and they kept the second passover feast there. This was one year after they left Egypt, 9.5. Then they travelled for 38 years through the desert and finally arrived at the edge of the land of Canaan. Deuteronomy contains a record of what Moses said to the people of Israel, and in Joshua, God brought them into the land He had promised them.

Moses wrote the book of Numbers, 33.2. The Lord Jesus told about the snake of brass that Moses had put up on a pole, 21.9; John 3.14. This shows that these things really happened and we can be sure the book of Numbers is the Word of God.

1/1   The fourth book of Moses is called NUMBERS because it tells us that the people of Israel were counted twice: before they started their journey through the desert, chapter 1, and again before they entered the land of Canaan, chapter 26. In this book we read about the journeys of the people of Israel from Mount Sinai to the border of the land of Canaan. When we come to the end of chapter 12 we see that the people had reached the desert of Paran at the southern border of the land and stayed for a while at Kadesh, 13.26. Moses then sent twelve men to see what the land was like, but the people refused to go in, chapter 14. God had promised to give the land of Canaan to the people of Israel, and He was angry with them when they did not believe that He would fulfil His promise. He punished them by making them walk around in the desert for 38 more years, 14.33. Finally they returned again to Kadesh, 20.1, and were ready to enter the land.

So we can divide the book of Numbers into three parts:
1. From Mount Sinai to Kadesh, chapters 1-12
2. From Kadesh through the desert and back to Kadesh, chapters 13-19
3. From Kadesh to Canaan, chapters 20-36

The people of Israel traveled part of the time and part of the time they wandered. These two things are not the same. It was God's will that Israel should travel through the desert to the land of Canaan, the land of promise. In the book of Numbers God told them where the men of each tribe should put their tents in the camp, chapter 2, and in what order they should march through the desert, chapter 3. A cloud protected them day and night. God provided everything they needed. When they obeyed God, He helped them to overcome their enemies. When they disobeyed, God judged them and made them *wander* in the desert for 38 years. It was not easy to wander around like this. They did not try to get to any special place, and these hard years were completely wasted. They went from place to place, but got no nearer to the land which God had promised to give them.

In the New Testament Christians are called strangers and travelers, 1 Peter 2.11. As strangers we are not at home in this world, but look forward to getting to our Father's house in heaven, John 14.2. As travelers we know where we want to go. It is never God's will for His people to live without any definite purpose or aim.

1/2 We have already seen that Numbers is the fourth book in the Bible. In the Scriptures *four* is the number which speaks of this world. In Genesis we read about the beginning of everything and in Exodus we see that the people of God were delivered out of Egypt. In Leviticus we see how they should worship God and in Numbers how they travelled through this *world*.

FROM SINAI TO KADESH, chapters 1-12

What do we read about in the first part of Numbers, chapters 1-12?

The people were numbered or counted for the first time, chapter 1.

God told them how the different tribes should travel, chapters 2-4.

Rules for special offerings, chapters 5,6.

Aaron and the Levites begin their service in the Tabernacle, chapters 7, 8.

The people went to Kadesh-barnea, chapters 9-12.

The people of Israel were counted the first time, chapter 1

1/3 One whole year and one month had passed since the people of Israel had left Egypt. On the first day of the second month God told Moses to count how many soldiers there were among them. He wanted one man from each tribe, the leader of the tribe, to help Moses in this work, 1.1-16.

On the very same day Moses and these leaders called all the people together and counted the soldiers among them, 1.17-47. They had to be at least 20 years old and be able to go to war. Jacob (Israel) had twelve sons, but in this chapter the Levites were not counted, and the two sons of Joseph were counted as two different tribes. In chapter 2 we will see the names of the chiefs of the different tribes and the number of soldiers in each tribe:

TRIBE	CHIEF	SOLDIERS
Reuben	Elizur, son of Shedeur	46,000
Simeon	Shelumiel, son of Zurishaddai	59,300
Judah	Nahshon, son of Amminadab	74,600
Issachar	Nethaneel, son of Zuar	54,400
Zebulun	Eliab, son of Helon	57,400
Ephraim	Elishama, son of Ammihud	40,500
Manasseh	Gamaliel, son of Pedahzur	32,200
Benjamin	Abidan, son of Gideoni	35,400
Dan	Ahiezer, son of Ammishaddai	62,700
Asher	Pagiel, son of Ocran	41,500
Gad	Eliasaph, son of Reuel	45,650
Naphthali	Ahira, son of Enan	53,400

We note that Judah was the largest tribe, but it did not become the most important tribe until the time of David. Joshua was of the tribe of Ephraim, 13.8. In the times of Joshua and the Judges the tribe of Ephraim was the most powerful of the twelve tribes.

1/4 The Levites were not counted with the soldiers of the other tribes. God gave them a better work, **1.48-54**. They were able to serve in the Tabernacle from the time they were 30 years old until they were 50, 4.3. There were 8,580 Levites between the ages of 30 and 50, and 22,000 more who were at least one month old, 4.48; 3.39.

In verse 37 of Exodus 12 we learned that there were about 600,000 men in Israel. The total given in Numbers 1.46 is 603,550. This is the same number as in Exodus 38.26 where the men each paid a half shekel of silver for the work of the Tabernacle. Moses did not count the men until the first day of the second month, but the money had been collected before then.

The lesson of this chapter is that the Lord knows those who are His people. They are all counted and written in His book. The Good Shepherd knows His sheep and calls them by name, John 10.3,14. All are important to Him. He knows everything that happens to them and none of them can ever be lost.

Order for the camp and for the journey, chapter 2

1/5 God told Moses where He wanted the people of each tribe to set up their tents around the Tabernacle, **2.1,2**. He also told him the order in which He wanted them to travel through the desert. The tribe of Judah and two smaller tribes, Issachar and Zebulun, were east of the Tabernacle. We also see the name of the captain of each tribe and the number of soldiers in the tribe, **vs.3-9**.

The tribes of Reuben, Simeon, and Gad were south of the Tabernacle, **2.10-16**. Ephraim, Manasseh and Benjamin were on the west side, **vs.18-24**, and on the north side Dan, Asher and Naphtali, **vs.25-32**.

1/6 This chapter also shows us the order in which God wanted the tribes to travel through the desert, vs.9,16,24,31. The Levites put their tents right around the Tabernacle in the middle of the camp, 3.23,29,35,38. In verses 17 and 21 of chapter 10 we will see which tribes went ahead of the Levites when the people of Israel travelled. These instructions show us that God wanted His people to walk in an orderly way through the desert.

We can see this same truth in the New Testament. God wants His people to do everything in an orderly way. It is important that we should do thing the way He has shown us in His Word and not the way we think is best. The New Testament tells us how to be saved. It also teaches us how Christians should walk in this world. Every Christian should be very careful to follow God's order in all things. Groups of Christians should do the same when they meet together to worship and serve God.

A road may seem right to a man, yet may end as the way to death, Proverbs 14.12.

The Levites, chapter 3

1/7 Aaron had four sons, but two of them died when they offered the wrong thing to the Lord, Leviticus 10.1,2. Eleazar and Ithamar served as priests with Aaron their father, **3.1-4**. God gave the whole tribe of Levi to Aaron to help in the work of the Tabernacle. Their work was to serve Aaron by looking after the Tabernacle, **vs.5-10**. The Lord took the Levites instead of the oldest son in every family, **vs.11-13**. When the people of Israel were still in Egypt, God had said that the oldest son in every family belonged to Him. They did not have to die, if blood had been put over the door of their houses, but still they belonged to God. God wanted these men to serve Him and look after the Tabernacle. He told Israel that He would take the men of Levi to do this instead of the oldest son of each family.

1/8 Now the Lord commanded Moses to count the men in the tribe of Levi, **3.14-16**. Levi had three sons, Gershon, Kohath, and Merari, **v.17**. These three men had eight sons, **vs.18-20**.

There were 7,500 men in the family of the Gershonites. Their chief was Eliasaph, the son of Lael, and their work was to look after the covers and the curtains or hangings of the Tabernacle. They put up their tents on the west side of the Tabernacle, **3.21-26.**

1/9 In the families of Kohath there were 8,600 men and their chief was Elizaphan, the son of Uzziel. They had to look after the furniture of the Tabernacle and the main curtain or veil. They put up their tents south of the Tabernacle. Eleazar, the son of Aaron, was over all the Levites and their chiefs, **3.27-32.**

There were 6,200 men in the families of Merari. Zuriel, the son of Abihail, was their chief and they put up their tents north of the Tabernacle. Their work was to care for the boards, bars, posts and supports which made up the walls of the Tabernacle, **3.33-37.** Moses and Aaron and Aaron's two sons put up their tents on the east side of the Tabernacle, **v.38.**

1/10 Moses counted all the oldest sons in Israel and found there were 22,273, **3.39-43.** The 22,000 men in the tribe of Levi took the place of 22,000 of the firstborn sons of the other tribes of Israel, and the people had to pay five shekels to redeem each of the other 273 men. God told Moses to give this money to Aaron and his sons, **3.44-51.**

We were slaves, slaves of sin, and under the judgment of death, like the oldest sons in Israel. We too have been delivered by blood, the blood of the Lord Jesus Christ, 1 Peter 1.18,19, and we belong to God. Now God wants us to serve Him with our whole lives, as the Levites did, 1 Corinthians 6.20.

Instructions for moving the Tabernacle, chapter 4

1/11 We already read in chapter 3 about the work of the three families of the Levites. In chapter 4 we learn more details about their work. Those who did this work had to be at least 30 years old and could not be older than 50, **4.1-3.**

When the cloud moved, God showed that He wanted the people to continue their journey, Exodus 40.36. Then the priest alone would go into the Tabernacle and cover the furniture (you can learn more about the Tabernacle and the things in it by reading "Studies in Exodus and Leviticus", pages 50-61, 66-70).

First the priests covered the ark with the Veil. Over this they put a covering of the skin of seals or porpoises. Then on top they laid a blue or violet cloth, **4.4-6.** They covered the table with a blue cloth and put the Bread and the dishes on the blue cloth; then they put a bright red cloth on top, then a seal skin cover, **vs.7,8.** The priests put a blue cloth and a seal skin cover on the lamp-stand, the gold altar, and other articles, **4.9-12.** The Kohathites carried all these things on wooden poles which were covered with gold, Exodus 25.13,28; 37.28.

Outside the tent there were two objects made of brass: the altar for burnt sacrifices and a large basin or laver. You can learn more about these in Exodus 27.1-8; 30.18-21. Here we read that the priest cleaned the altar and put a blue cloth on it, then laid the altar equipment on the cloth, and a seal skin covering on top, **4.13,14.** We do not read about the basin or laver, but probably the priests covered it and the Kohathites carried it in the same way on poles.

When the priests had covered all these things the Kohathites carried them as the people traveled. Eleazar was over all the Levites, **3.32; 4.16.**

1/12 The Kohathites were not allowed to see the holy things of the Tabernacle, but they could carry them without sinning, **4.17-20.**

The Gershonites carried the curtains, coverings, hangings, and instruments of the Tabernacle. The priests directed them in this service, **4.21-28.**

The families of Merari carried the boards, posts, supports, stands, pins and instruments. Ithamar, the son of Aaron, was over the work of the Gershonites and the Merarites, **4.29-33.**

1/13 The thick curtains were very heavy to carry, and so were the boards covered with gold and the furniture of the Tabernacle. However, there were thousands of men who could do this work, **4.34-49:**

Kohathites	2,750	*to carry the furniture*
Gershonites	2,630	*to carry the hangings and curtains*
Merarites	3,200	*to carry the boards and posts*
	8,580	

For long journeys they put the boards and curtains on carts which were pulled by oxen. However, the Kohathites had to carry the furniture on their shoulders.

God had given very exact instructions as to how His people should make the Tabernacle and how they should serve Him in it. He also told them just how they should move it from place to place. The tribes traveled through the desert in the right order as God had commanded them and they carried the Tabernacle with them in the way He told them.

Many years later King David told his men to put the ark on a cart in order to move it to another place, but God showed His anger very quickly, 2 Samuel 6. This world is like a desert and we Christians are traveling to our home in heaven. Let us try very hard to obey the commands of the Lord and to do exactly as He tells us to do. Let us please the Lord by following the Word of God instead of the ideas and customs of men.

God commanded the people to be holy, chapter 5

1/14 In the book of Numbers we see that God is a God of order. He told the different tribes where to put their tents in the camp and in what order they should travel. Now we read about lepers and people with open sores; they were called *unclean,* Leviticus 13.46; 15.2. Others were unclean because they touched a dead body, Leviticus 21.1; Numbers 19.11. They could not worship with all the people until they became clean again. Now the Lord commanded the Israelites to put these unclean people outside the camp, **5.1-4.** (See "Studies in Exodus and Leviticus", pages 103-106.)

The Lord had given instructions for the guilt offering in Leviticus 6.1-7. A man had to pay back what he had taken, and a fifth of the amount as well. Now we learn that this must be paid back even if the other man had died; the nearest relative would get it, **5.5-8.** However, every sacrifice for the Lord belongs to the priest, **vs.9, 10.**

1/15 How to test a woman if her husband thought she had committed sin, **5.11-31.** A man could bring an offering if he thought that his wife had not been faithful to him. The purpose of the offering was to tell if the woman was innocent or guilty. The offering was three pints of barly meal without oil or incense, **v.15**. The priest prepared bitter water for the test; he took dust from the floor of the Tabernacle and put it in clean water in a clay pot. The woman stood before the Lord with her head uncovered and the barly meal in her hands. The priest told her that the bitter water would not hurt her if she was innocent, but if she had sinned, the Lord would make her suffer so everyone would know. The bitter water would affect her body and this would show that she was guilty. The woman said "Amen" to show that she agreed with what the priest had said, **vs. 16-22**. Then the priest wrote these curses in a book and washed them out with a little bitter water, **v.23**. The woman had to drink some of the water, **v.24**. Then the priest took the meal offering and burned a handful of it on the altar, and made the woman drink more of the water, **vs.25,26**.

If the woman was innocent she would be able to have children even after drinking the bitter water. If she was guilty everyone would know it and the people would use her name as a curse, **5.27**.

Why did God give this law? He wanted to keep His people from committing this sin of adultery, but if a woman was innocent, her husband should not be jealous of her, **5.28**.

Why do we read only about the woman here and not the man? The man was the head of the home and it was his duty to see that the members of his family lived the way they should. He must find out the truth if he thought his wife had sinned.

No family can be happy if the husband or wife is jealous of the other, or thinks the other is guilty of immorality. If a person is guilty God will punish him or her. But if the person is not guilty, there should be no jealousy among the members of the family to spoil their happiness. In Israel the Lord provided this test so that a man would not think his wife was guilty if she was innocent, and so that her sin would not be hidden if she was really guilty.

There is another reason for mentioning only the wife here. This reason is that the wife is a picture of the Church, the Bride of Christ. Of course our Lord and Master never sinned and He knows everything. We should remember this; it will keep us from thinking or saying or doing anything that would make Him unhappy.

Nazirites, chapter 6

1/16 God gave His law to the people of Israel. In this law He commanded them to bring certain offerings and to give to the Lord one part out of ten of everything they received. God also said that anyone could bring other offerings just because he loved the Lord. He might bring peace offerings or burnt offerings just because he himself wanted to, not because the Law said he must do so.

A believer might be sick and promise to give something to the Lord if he got well again. This might be something he owned, an animal or someone in his family; or he might promise to give himself to the Lord. You can read more about these things in Leviticus 27.

Some people promised God to become Nazirites. They promised to give a number of weeks or months to Jehovah.

During this time the Nazirite stopped doing his own work and put himself apart to serve God, **6.1,2,8**. He could not drink wine nor eat the fruit of the vine, **vs.3,4**. He had to let his hair grow long to show that he had set himself apart for God, **v.5**. Long hair is usually disgraceful for a man, 1 Corinthians 11.14. The Nazirite could not touch a dead person; he could not help to bury anyone, even someone who belonged to his own family. He was *holy to the Lord* in a very special way, **vs.6-8**. If someone suddenly died beside him, he had to shave the hair off his head, wait for seven days and then shave it again. The following day he had to bring two birds for a sin offering and a burnt offering, and a lamb for a guilt offering. Then he had to start again from the beginning and keep the full number of days which he had promised to God, **vs.9-12**.

1/17 When this time was finished, the Nazirite brought his offering to the Lord: a male lamb one year old for a burnt offering, a female lamb one year old for a sin offering, together with the meal and drink offerings according to the Law. For a peace offering he brought a male goat and a basket full of bread made without yeast, **6.13-17**. At the door of the Tabernacle the Nazirite shaved his head and burned the hair in the fire. At the same time the priest burned parts of his peace offering, but the rest of the peace offering was for the priest himself. When the Nazirite had finished all these things, he could drink wine again and live a normal life, **vs.18-20.** The Nazirite brought all these offerings according to the Law; he could bring others also if he wanted to, but he must bring these at least, **v.21.**

Why did these things please God? Because they pointed forward to His Son, the Lord Jesus Christ. The Lord set Himself completely apart for God. He lived His whole life here on earth humbly and sacrificially and entirely separate from all sin and everything which was unclean.

We read about Samson's parents who set him apart to God to be a Nazirite from the day he was born, Judges 13.5; but Samson was weak and he did not live the way a Nazirite should, Judges 16.17. Later the people of Jerusalem rejected God and gave wine to the Nazirites, Amos 2.12. So the Nazirites did not do all that God had commanded them to do because their **own people** stopped them. In the time of the prophet Jeremiah the enemies of Judah took the city of Jerusalem. They prevented the people for a while from worshipping Jehovah and they persecuted the Nazirites, Lamentations 4.7,8. At that time the **enemies** kept the Nazirites from doing what they should have done. The Lord Jesus did not have a sinful nature and He was never weak like Samson, so weakness never kept Him from doing what is right. His own people and His enemies persecuted Him, but He always did everything that God wanted Him to do.

Today all true Christians are Nazirites. We should not try to live like rich and proud people but should give our lives completely to the Lord. Many young people use their school vacation to serve the Lord. Others take one or two years of their lives and give themselves wholly to the work of the Lord for that time. After that some return to their work again and live as they did before, but others continue to use all their time to serve God. The Holy Spirit wants us to offer our bodies as a living sacrifice to God, set apart to serve and to please Him, Romans 12.1.

Then the Lord told Moses how Aaron should bless the people of Israel, **6.22-27**. Aaron was to pray in these words:

1. "The Lord bless you" - this gives in short form everything else in the prayer.

2. "The Lord watch and keep you" - so you won't get away from Him, or sin against Him, or start following the enemy.

3. "The Lord make His face shine on you" - this means the same as "the Lord look kindly on you." Both mean "the Lord be gracious to you."

4. "and give you peace" - peace with God, peace in the camp, peace with your enemies.

The Lord showed that the people of Israel were His people when He put His own name on them and promised to bless them, 6.27.

In the New Testament we read that we are blessed with all spiritual gifts in the heavenly world through our union with Christ, Ephesians 1.3. The apostle Paul prayed for the saints according to the will of God, Ephesians 1.15-23; 3.14-21. This shows us a little of how the Lord Jesus, our Great High Priest, is praying for us. In John 17 the Lord Jesus gave us an example of how He prays for us. We can pray for other believers or the Lord's servants and this makes us like Him who lives forever to pray for us, Hebrews 7.25.

TEST YOURSELF - Numbers chapters 1-6

1. Why is the fourth book in the Bible called Numbers?
2. Where did Israel travel in the first part of the book?
3. How many months passed from the time Israel left Egypt to the time Moses counted them?
4. Why did Moses count the Levites separately from the other tribes?
5. Which were the four main tribes?
6. What lesson can we learn from chapter 2?
7. The oldest son in every family belonged to the Lord. Whom did the Lord choose instead of the oldest sons?
8. There were not enough Levites to make up for all the oldest sons; how much did the people pay for the other 273 men?
9. What did the people see on top of the ark, the table, lamp stand, the gold altar and the brass altar?
10. Who carried these things through the desert?
11. What happened when David did not follow these instructions?
12. A man should pay back anything he had taken from another. What did he do if the other man died?
13. What happens in a family where someone is jealous of another?
14. Why did the Nazirite let his hair grow long?
15. Name one Nazirite who failed. Why did he fail?
16. Who is our Great High Priest who is always praying for us?

Turn to page 145 to check your answers.

SINAI TO KADESH 2

1/18 The priests began to worship God in the Tabernacle while the nation was still at Mount Sinai. After that the people of Israel travelled through the desert to Kadesh-barnea on the border of the land of Canaan.

THE PRIESTS BEGAN TO USE THE TABERNACLE
chapters 7, 8

In Exodus we read how Moses built the Tabernacle; now we see that the priests began to use it for worshipping God.

The offerings of the twelve captains, chapter 7

The Tabernacle was set up on the first day of the first month of the second year after the people of Israel had left Egypt, Exodus 40.17. At that time the captains of the twelve tribes brought six carts and twelve oxen as an offering to the Lord, **7.1-3**. God told Moses to accept these gifts, **vs.4,5**.

Moses gave two carts and four oxen to the Gershonites, to carry the heavy curtains of the Tabernacle. To the Merarites he gave four carts and eight oxen, to carry the boards, **7.6-8**. God had commanded the Kohathites to carry the furniture of the Tabernacle on their shoulders, **v.9**, so they did not receive any of the carts.

1/19 The twelve captains also offered sacrifices for the altar, **7.10-89**. We saw the names of these men before in chapter 2. Each one gave exactly the same offering:

1. For a meal offering: a silver dish which weighed 3 pounds, 4 ounces, a silver bowl which weighed 1 pound, 12 ounces, both full of fine flour mixed with oil; a gold saucer or large spoon which weighed 4 ounces and was full of incense.

2. For a whole burnt offering: one bull, one male sheep and one lamb.

3. For a sin offering: one young goat.
4. For a peace offering: two oxen, five male sheep, five male goats, and five lambs.

All these sacrifices were added up in verses 84-88.

1/20 Why did God lead Moses to write down the offering of each captain separately even though all the offerings were exactly the same? God values equally all gifts from His children and He told Moses that each captain should bring his offering on a different day, 7.11. This is the first time we read of anyone bringing an offering which God had not commanded, after the Tabernacle was set up. Since that time thousands of Israelites have brought their offerings to Jehovah and these offerings were all equally precious to Him.

1/21 In this chapter we can also see pictures of Christ. The gold reminds us that He is God, and the silver that He died to redeem us. The flour mixed with oil is a picture of the perfect life He lived here in this world in the power of the Holy Spirit. This was pleasing to God like the sweet smell of incense. All the sacrifices speak of the death of the Lord Jesus Christ on the cross. God loves to hear about His Son. The New Testament tells us that the Christians came together on the first day of the week to remember the Lord. We can praise the Lord Jesus Christ at all times, for the Father never gets tired of listening to His children when they speak well of His beloved Son.

1/22 In the last verse of chapter 7 the Lord spoke to Moses from the cover of the Ark in the Most Holy Place. We should notice how these different things follow each other. At the beginning of the book of Numbers we saw where the different tribes should put up their tents and in what order they should travel. In chapter 6 we read first about the Nazirites who set themselves apart for God because they loved Him and then how the high priest should bless the people. Then the captains, representing the people, brought sacrifices just because they themselves wanted to do so. After this God told Moses more about Himself, **7.89**.

From this we learn a very important truth: We should obey what God has already told us to do; then He will tell us more of His perfect plan for us. Do you want God to bless you? There is only one way: you must obey immediately everything He tells you to do.

Aaron lighted the lamps, 8.1-4

1/23 In Exodus 40 we read how Moses set up the Tabernacle and put everything in its right place. He anointed all the different things with oil to show that they were holy to the Lord. Then in verses 24 and 25 we see that he lit the lamps. Here in Numbers 8.1-4 we read more details about the lamps.

The Levites began their service, 8.5-26

The Lord commanded Moses to cleanse the Levites and to get them ready for their service in the Tabernacle. He put a few drops of some special water on them, Numbers 19.9. They had to shave their whole bodies and wash their clothes. For a burnt offering they brought a young bull with the meal offering and oil to go with it; and for a sin offering they brought another young bull. The leaders of the people of Israel laid their hands on the Levites, and Aaron presented them before the Lord as a special gift from the Israelites. Then the Levites laid their hands on the bulls which were offered to the Lord. The Lord claimed the Levites for His service instead of the first-born sons of the other tribes. God then gave them to the priests to serve in the Tabernacle in place of the people of Israel, **8.5-19**.

1/24 Moses and the Levites obeyed these commands of the Lord, and then the Levites began their service in the Tabernacle, **8.20-22**.

The Levites had to be between 25 years and 50 years old in order to serve the Lord in this way. In 4.35 we saw that they did not carry any burdens before they were 30 years old. When the Levites were over 50 years old they could still serve in the court of the Tabernacle, and protect it, 1.53, but they did not have to lift heavy curtains or boards any more, **8.23-26**.

The Levites did the work of the Tabernacle in the place of the people of Israel. Today it is not right for one Christian to serve the Lord in the place of another Christian. **Every true Christian should understand that his whole life belongs to the Lord and every Christian should serve the Lord.** Some can give all their time to preaching the Good News and teaching the Word of God. Others work and earn money to supply what their families need and to help those who give themselves entirely to the work of God. Every one of us should understand that we belong completely to the Lord and we should serve and glorify Him, 1 Corinthians 6.20.

THE JOURNEY TO KADESH — chapters 9-12

In these chapters we will see how Israel travelled through the desert. But first we will learn about the Passover, the cloud and the silver trumpets.

The second Passover, 9.1-14

/25 At the beginning of the book of Numbers we read what happened on the first day of the second month of the second year after the people of Israel left Egypt. In **9.1-5** we see that the Lord had commanded Moses to keep the Passover on the fourteenth day of the *first* month. The people had done this, but some of them had not been able to eat the Passover with the others because they were *unclean* at that time. They had touched a dead body and that made them unclean. These men asked if there was some way they could bring their offering to the Lord just the same. Moses asked the Lord about this problem, **vs.6-8**. He learned that God would accept two reasons which might prevent an Israelite from keeping the Passover: (1) he had touched a dead body and was unclean; (2) he was away on a long journey. God would allow him to keep the Passover a month later, on the fourteenth day of the *second* month, **vs.9-12**. Anyone who failed to keep the Passover for any other reason had to die. God commanded that strangers living with the people of Israel must also die if they did not keep the Passover, **vs.13,14**.

It is always easy to excuse ourselves from obeying God's commands, but we should ask ourselves if God will accept our excuses. If we really love the Lord we will look for opportunities to serve and please Him, and not try to make excuses.

The cloud, 9.15-23

1/26 When the Tabernacle was set up, the cloud covered it, Exodus 40.34. The people could see this cloud in the day time and at night the cloud was bright like fire over the Tabernacle. The cloud proved that the Lord was there with them. It also showed the people of Israel when they should travel and where they should go. In these nine verses we read six times that the people travelled only when the Lord told them to do so, 9.17,18, 20,21,22,23, and six times that the Lord told them when they should set up their tents again, vs.17,18,19,20,22,23. They moved only when the Lord commanded them.

> This is very important. We too should let the Lord guide us in our journey through this world to our heavenly home. We do not have a cloud, but we have the Holy Scriptures and the Holy Spirit. Every believer should ask the Lord to guide him. There are many verses in the Bible to show us God's will for us every day. In addition the Holy Spirit is able to guide those who obey Him. We should ask the Lord to direct us in even the smallest details of our lives.

The silver trumpets, 10.1-10

1/27 The Lord commanded Moses to make two silver trumpets and the priests used these in the desert.

They blew both trumpets, to call all the people together.

They blew one trumpet, to call only the princes together.

They blew both trumpets for a longer time: this meant that the tribes to the east of the Tabernacle (Judah, Issachar, Zebulun) should go forward.

They blew both trumpets again: this meant that the tribes south of the Tabernacle (Reuben, Simeon, Gad) should go forward, then the other tribes also in order.

In the land of Canaan the priests were to use the trumpets to declare war against an enemy. They blew them also when the sacrifices were made on feast days and on the first day of each month.

> We are always fighting against our enemy, the devil, but we look forward to the day when we will hear the sound of a

trumpet. At that time we will meet our Lord in the air, and from then on we will be with Him forever, 1 Thessalonians 4.16,17. After that seven trumpets will sound in heaven. These trumpets will announce the terrible judgment that God will pour out on unbelievers during the Great Tribulation, Revelation 8.6 - 9.21; 11.15-19.

In the first few chapters of Numbers we read how God prepared the people for their journey through the desert. He commanded Moses to count the people and showed him where the different tribes should put up their tents in the camp. He also showed Moses in what order the tribes should travel, and how the Nazirites and the Levites should serve Him. Moses and the people obeyed these commands faithfully. The Lord also gave them the cloud to show them when they should start to travel, in what direction they should go, and when they should stop. We can be sure that God has given us everything we need to walk in the right way. If we read His Word, we cannot lose our way, if we are willing to obey.

So in Numbers 1.1-10.10 we have the history of Israel and what the Lord commanded them to do while they were still at Mount Sinai. Now they began to travel through the desert, and soon reached Kadesh-barnea, chapter 13. For 38 years they wandered through the desert and in chapter 19 got back to Kadesh. The rest of Numbers tells about their journey to the border of the land of Canaan, chapters 20-36.

The first part of the journey, 10.11-36

1/28 The guiding cloud rose up from the Tabernacle on the twentieth day of the second month of the second year. The people of Israel folded up their tents and moved to the desert of Paran. The cloud showed them that God wanted them to stay there for a while, **10.11,12**.

In 2.9,16,24 and 31 we saw the order which the tribes were to follow when they travelled. Now we see the tribe of Judah went first, with Issachar and Zebulun. The Gershonites and the Merarites took down the Tabernacle and followed these three tribes, **10.13-17**. The Kohathites carried the furniture of the Tabernacle and followed the tribes of Reuben, Simeon and Gad, vs.18-21. The rest of the tribes made up the camps of Ephraim and Dan and followed in order, vs.22-28. However some of the Kohathites carried the ark and went before all the Israelites to lead the way, v.33.

1/29 Jethro, Moses' father-in-law, came to visit him while Israel was still at Mount Sinai, Exodus 18. Now we read about Hobab, the son of Raguel or Reuel, another name for Jethro. Moses asked Hobab to stay with them and share in the blessings the Lord had promised to give the people of Israel, 10.29-32. Hobab refused, so Moses asked him to be their guide and lead them through the desert. Moses should have trusted God, who was guiding them with the cloud. We do not read about Hobab again in the Bible, but the Lord was certainly able to guide Israel.

So they left Mount Sinai and travelled on. The ark went in front of them, **10.33**, and the cloud protected them in the day time, **v.34**. Moses prayed to the Lord to take care of the people when they travelled, **v.35**, and when they found a place to camp, **v.36**.

Both the ark and cloud showed that Jehovah was with His people, but Moses also prayed the Lord to protect them. Today the Holy Spirit lives in all true believers. Still God wants us to ask Him to care for us and to protect us, and He wants us to thank Him when He has answered our prayers.

The people of Israel complained against God, chapter 11

1/30 God had given Israel everything they needed for their first journey from Mount Sinai, but they began to complain very soon. We do not read what they complained about but their grumbling displeased the Lord and He sent fire to punish them, **11.1-3**.

Moses called this place *Taberah* so that the people would remember what had happened, but they soon forgot the lesson the Lord had tried to teach them. In Exodus 12.38 we saw that all kinds of people left Egypt together with Israel. These may have been Egyptians who did not really believe in Jehovah, or perhaps their fathers were Egyptians and their mothers were women of Israel. These men remembered the food they used to eat in Egypt and the people of Israel began to weep because they wanted meat to eat. They really wanted the pleasures of Egypt, 11.5, and hated the food that God had given them. Every morning Jehovah performed a miracle and provided the manna for them and they could cook it in different ways, 11.4-9.

God had promised before to give them meat to eat, and He had already fulfilled this promise at least once, Exodus 16.8,13. The people should have asked God for what they needed and believed that He would supply, but instead of doing that they complained bitterly.

Satan always tries to make men think that God does not love them. He did this to Eve, Genesis 3.1; and he will do it to us.

The Lord became angry again and this made Moses unhappy also. But this time Moses himself began to complain against the Lord; he said God did not give him enough strength for his work. Both Moses and the people said that God had not given them enough, but Moses' sin was greater because he was closer to the Lord. He became so discouraged that he asked God to kill him, 11.10-15.

2/1 God was gracious to Moses and promised to give the Holy Spirit to seventy of the elders of Israel. These men would then be able to share with Moses the work which he thought was too great for him alone. At Mount Sinai Moses had listened to the advice of his father-in-law and had appointed judges for groups of one thousand people, groups of one hundred, fifty, and ten people, Exodus 18.25. This may have been wise according to man's wisdom, but now the time had come when it was God's will to appoint seventy older men to help Moses, 11.16,17.

It is always better to wait for God to act than to listen to men's advice.

God also promised the meat which the people demanded. They had asked for it, but did not really believe that God would give it to them. Now God agreed to answer their prayer but He said He would judge them because they had not believed. He said they would eat meat for a whole month, until they were tired of it. Moses could not understand where all this meat would come from and it was very difficult for him to believe. He asked if they should kill all the cattle or if God would bring all the fish of the sea together for them. The Lord rebuked Moses and told him that He had all power and would fulfill His promise, **11.18-23**.

The Holy Spirit may use these verses to rebuke us too, if we are tempted to doubt that God will really do what He has promised.

2/2 First God provided what Moses needed, men to help him. The Holy Spirit came on seventy older men and they began to prophesy, **11.24,25**. Most of them were near the Tabernacle which at that time was outside the camp, but the Spirit came on two of them who had stayed in the camp, and they prophesied also, **v.26**. Joshua heard about this and wanted Moses to tell them to stop, **vs.27,28**. He was afraid that people would not honour Moses if others could also speak for God.

Thoughts like these cause trouble among Christians. It is very easy for us to be jealous when the Lord gives our work to someone else. Moses had sinned when he complained against the Lord, v.15, and when he did not believe God's promise, v.22, but he was not jealous. He would have been happy if all the Lord's people had the Spirit of God and could prophesy. In verse 14 he had felt very badly about the people, but now his heart was again full of love for them, **11.29**.

The Bible says that prophecy is the greatest gift, 1 Corinthians 14.1. It is very important for every child of God to know the Scriptures well so that he can explain God's message to others, 1 Peter 3.15.

Then God gave the people what **they** wanted. He sent a very great flock of quails to provide meat for the people. They collected these birds for two days and a night until every person had a large number of them, at least 10 homers each. However as soon as they started to eat the meat they became very sick and many of them died. Moses called that place Kibroth-hattaavah, which means "the graves of greed", **11.30-35**.

Psalm 78.17-31 also tells about what happened at Kibroth-hattaavah. It is a terrible sin to complain about what God has provided for us and to covet the things of this world. The Lord commands us not to complain as the Israelites did, 1 Corinthians 10.10. In Philippians He told us to do all things without complaining. We should ask God for what we need and at the same time thank Him for all His goodness to us, Philippians 2.14; 4.6. We should also ask Him to give us only what is according to His will; this is how the Lord Himself prayed, Luke 22.42.

Aaron and Miriam were jealous of Moses, chapter 12

2/3 Now Satan tried to divide the people of Israel by working through some of their leaders. He knows that God's people can not enjoy the blessing of the Lord if they are fighting among themselves. We have just seen that Moses was very humble and really cared for the people, 11.29. Now Miriam and Aaron blamed Moses because he had married a woman from Cush or Ethiopia. Zipporah was Moses' first wife, Exodus 2.21, but perhaps she had died. Maybe Moses' sister and brother thought he should have married a woman of Israel. However in verse 2 we see the real reason why they were angry with him. They thought they could speak for God with as much authority as Moses.

We believe that Moses wrote the book of Numbers, but how could any man use the words of verse 3 without being proud? Of course no one can be proud and humble at the same time. Perhaps Joshua added verse 3. (It may be that the Holy Spirit also led him or someone else to write the last chapter of Deuteronomy, which tells that Moses died and was buried.) However it is also possible that the Spirit told Moses to write these words and that he could do so without feeling proud. Our Lord Jesus could say that He was humble and of course saying this was not a sin, Matthew 11.29. The Lord was only saying what the prophet had written about the Messiah, Zechariah 9.9.

It is sin not to accept what God's Word says about us. For example, the Bible says we can know that we have eternal life, 1 John 5.13, so it is not pride for me to say I know this. It would be sin to say that I am not sure.

God quickly defended Moses, His faithful servant. He commanded Moses and Aaron and Miriam to come out to the

Tabernacle. The cloud came down and the Lord told Aaron and Miriam that Moses was closer to Him than any ordinary prophet. God spoke with Moses face to face, and Miriam and Aaron should have been afraid to speak against him, 12.4-8.

2/4 Then the cloud moved from the tent and Aaron saw that Miriam had the disease of leprosy in her skin. Aaron confessed immediately that they had sinned and Moses asked God to heal Miriam again. However the Lord said Miriam should first stay outside the camp for a week. He wanted all the people to learn that they must not be jealous of Moses or speak against him, 12.9-16.

In this chapter we see that Moses was humble, v.3; faithful, v.7; and willing to forgive, v.13. Let us follow his example.

This chapter also teaches us that leaders must be especially careful not to sin. A leader who sins should be rebuked in front of all the people of the church, 1 Timothy 5.20.

THE ORDER OF THE TRIBES

AS THEY WALKED THROUGH THE DESERT

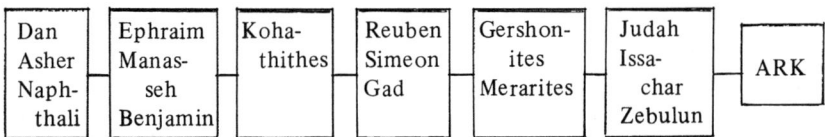

TEST YOURSELF - Numbers chapters 7-12

1. Why did Moses not give any carts to the Kohathites?
2. How many animals did each chief give as sacrifices?
3. Why did the Holy Spirit lead Moses to write down all these details twelve times?
4. What can we learn from Numbers 7.89?
5. What tribe did God give to Aaron to serve him instead of all the first born sons?
6. What could the Levites do between the ages of 25 and 30?
7. Give one reason which God would accept if a man failed to keep the Passover.
8. Why did the priests blow the silver trumpets in Canaan?
9. Who went first when Israel walked through the desert?
10. Which verse shows Moses' faith, 10.31 or 10.35?
11. How did God answer the people when they grumbled? 11.4-6
12. How did God answer Moses' complaint? 12.15
13. How did Moses show he really loved the people?
14. Did Moses write Numbers 12.3?

Turn to page 145 to check your answers

ISRAEL REBELLED AT KADESH-BARNEA   3

2/5 The people of Israel left Sinai, 10.12, then Hazeroth, 12.16, and came to Kadesh in the desert of Paran, 13.26. This place is called Kadesh-barnea in Deuteronomy 1.19 and is very important in the history of Israel. It is on the border of the land which God had promised to give Israel. The people could have entered the land right away if they had obeyed the Lord. However they did not believe God's promises or obey His commands. Because of this they had to wander in the desert for 38 more years.

Kadesh-barnea reminds us that we must all make decisions. We should get into the habit of obeying the Lord's commands at once. Then we will make the right decision when we suddenly have to choose.

Moses sent men to explore the land, chapter 13

The Lord commanded Moses to send a man from each tribe to explore the land of Canaan and see what it was like, **13.1,2**. Later we learn that the people themselves had asked for this, Deuteronomy 1.22,23. Joshua was one of the twelve men whom Moses chose. He was also called Oshea or Jehoshua and belonged to the tribe of Ephraim. Moses also chose Caleb who went to represent the tribe of Judah, **vs.3-16**.

2/6 Moses commanded these twelve leaders to see if the land was good and if the people in it were strong, **13.17-20**. Why did he want to know these things? God had already told them that it was a good land, Exodus 3.8. He had promised to give it to Israel even if the people of the land were very strong. In Ezekiel 20.6 we see that God had already examined the land and they did not need to do so again. Moses also told them to bring some of the fruit of the land. The people of Israel had been thinking about the fruit of Egypt, **11.5**, but Moses was looking forward to the fruit of the Promised Land, the land of Canaan.

The twelve men explored the land thoroughly. Kadesh-barnea is on the south border of the land and they went all the way to Rehob which is in the north at the other end of the country. At Hebron they saw the people of Anak and at Eshcol they cut a branch with one large bunch of grapes, and also got some other fruit, **13.21-25**.

Then they went back to Moses and said that the land was wonderful. They told Moses that they had brought back some of the fruit to prove that they were telling the truth. They also said that the people of the land were strong and that the cities had great walls around them, **13.26-29**.

2/7   Caleb said that the Israelites would be able to defeat the people of Canaan, **13.30**, but the other men did not agree with him at all. They said that the people of Canaan were stronger than Israel and that their land was not good, but would swallow up the people who live in it. They said that they themselves looked very small, as small as grasshoppers, and the people of the land were like giants, **vs.31-33**.

It is true that there were giants on the earth before the flood, but these all died in the waters of the flood, Genesis 6.4. In the old Hebrew Bible the word "giants" is used only here and in Genesis 6.4. Verse 33 shows us that these men did not believe God at all. They were very much afraid and so they thought the people of the land were much greater than they really were. They made the people of Israel believe that the land was bad and the people in it terribly tall.

The people of Israel rebelled against God, chapter 14

2/8   The people wept all night after they heard the report of the spies. They wished they had died in Egypt or in the desert and said that God had brought them to Canaan so that they might die there, **14.1-3**. They even chose a man to be their captain and lead them back to Egypt, **v.4**; Nehemiah 9.17.

Moses and Aaron threw themselves to the ground in front of all the people who had gathered together. Joshua and Caleb tried to tell the people again that the land was good and that the Lord would help them defeat their enemies, **14.5-9**. Their words made the people still more angry. They wanted to kill Joshua and Caleb with stones, but the Lord saved them. In 12.10 the cloud had left the Tabernacle, but now God's glory appeared again, **v.10**.

2/9 The people made God angry because they did not believe Him or obey His commands. At first He warned them that He would kill them through sickness and make the descendants of Moses into another nation, **14.11,12**. God spoke in this way once before, Exodus 32.10, but Moses had prayed for the people. Now Moses asked the Lord again to forgive the sin of Israel. He did not want the other nations to say that God was not **able** to bring them into the land of Canaan. Moses knew that God was a God of mercy, and so he begged Him to forgive His people, **vs.13-19**.

God answered Moses' prayer and said that He would not destroy the people at that time, but they would all die in the desert. They themselves had wished this before, v.2. God could forgive them because Moses had prayed for them, but He had to punish them also, **14.20-25**.

We can see this also in the life of David. David confessed his sin and God forgave him, but He had to punish David too, 2 Samuel 12.13,14. Even today God forgives Christians who confess their sins, 1 John 1.9, but they must also bear the results of their sins in this world.

This is the tenth time that the people grumbled against God and put Him to the test. We will list here the other nine times. They grumbled or disobeyed God when:

1. they were afraid of the Egyptians, Exodus 14.11.
2. they had only bitter water to drink, Exodus 15.24.
3. they were hungry, Exodus 16.2,3.
4. they were afraid that God would not give them manna every day, Exodus 16.20.
5. they thought that the manna would not stay fresh over the sabbath day, Exodus 16.27,28.
6. they were thirsty, Exodus 17.3.

7. they had a desire to worship idols, Exodus 32.1.
8. they thought they had a lot of trouble, Numbers 11.1.
9. they wanted meat to eat, Numbers 11.4.

/10 In some ways the people acted worse at Kadesh-barnea than they had ever done before. We can read about this also in Hebrews 3.7-11. God did not force them to go into the land while they did not believe Him, and so they had to die in the desert, **14.26-30**. They thought that God would not protect their children, but God said that the children would enter the land after their parents had died, **vs.31-33**. Only two of the adults living at that time would go into the land, Joshua and Caleb, vs.24,30. The twelve men had spent 40 *days* in the land of Canaan to see what it was like. They did so because they did not really believe what God had already told them about the land. Now the nation of Israel would have to wander 40 *years* in the desert because they did not believe God's promises, **vs.34,35**. These ten men were destroyed immediately, **vs.36-38**.

The people were very sorry when Moses told them these things. They did not want to spend another 38 years in the desert and so they changed their minds and got ready to go into the land at once. Moses told them not to fight with the Amalekites and the Canaanites because the Lord was not with them. They went anyway, but the enemy defeated them, **14.39-45**.

This chapter teaches us some very important lessons:
1. Listen only to those leaders who tell you to obey God's word.
2. Ask God to show you His will every time you have to make an important decision.
3. When you have great problems remember that God's power is still greater.
4. When God punishes you, accept the punishment humbly and try to learn the lessons He wants to teach you.
5. Do not try to do anything in your own strength.

Rules for those who would enter the land, chapter 15

?/11 In chapter 14 we saw how the people of Israel rebelled against God and how God had to punish them because they disobeyed. In chapter 16 we will read about Korah who led others to rebel against God again. Between these two sad chapters the Holy Spirit gives us some beautiful pictures about the One who never rebelled against His Father, the Lord Jesus Christ.

God said that the adults would never enter the land of Canaan. This showed that He was *righteous.* In **15.1-13** He gave commands for those who *would* enter. This showed that He was also *gracious.* Twice in this chapter He spoke of what they were to do when they would enter the land, vs.2,18. In this way God showed that the nation of Israel would finally have the land of promise even if many of the people had to die in the desert before that time.

God told those who would enter the land that they should offer flour, oil and wine with their burnt offerings and their peace offerings. They had to offer these things in different amounts depending on whether the main sacrifice was a lamb, a ram or a bull.

Animal	Flour	Oil	Wine
Lamb	2 quarts	1½ pints	1½ pints
Ram	4 quarts	2 pints	2 pints
Bull	6 quarts	3 pints	3 pints
Death of Christ	*Life of Christ*	*Holy Spirit*	*Believer's Joy*

2/12 These rules were for the people of Israel and also for the people of other nations who lived with them. People from other nations could offer sacrifices to God, but they had to obey the same rules, **15.14-16**.

An Israelite who offered a large sacrifice is like a believer who thinks very much of Christ. The fine flour speaks of Christ as a Man and the animal that was killed is a picture of the Lord's death on the cross. The oil is a picture of the Holy Spirit and the wine is a picture of joy. The Israelites had to offer larger amounts of flour, oil and wine with the bigger sacrifices. In the same way, our joy will be greater if we think more of Christ and of His sacrifice for us, if we love Him more, and if we allow the Holy Spirit to work in and through us.

We can study God's Word and learn more about Christ. We can understand better how important His death was, and worship Him more. This is like an Israelite who brought a large animal to show that he loved God.

At the same time we will learn more about the perfect life of Christ and the work of the Holy Spirit. Our joy will keep on growing too.

In Leviticus 23.10 God told His people to bring Him an offering of grain from their fields right at the beginning of the harvest. After they had entered the land they should take some grain and present it before the Lord. At the same time they should offer a burnt offering and a meal offering. Now in Numbers 15 the Lord told them to bring a special offering when they first made their bread, **15.17-21**.

After that He told them again what they should do if they sinned without knowing it. If the whole nation sinned against the Lord they had to bring a bull for a burnt offering and a goat for a sin offering. If one person sinned without knowing it, he had to bring a female goat for a sin offering, **15.22-29**.

In these verses we see again and again that these sacrifices were only for those who sinned without knowing it. They were not to be offered by people who knew what was wrong and did it just the same. There was no sacrifice in the law of Moses which people could offer for doing something that they knew to be a sin. A person who sinned purposely was to be cut off from the nation of Israel, **15.30,31**.

2/13 One time a man collected sticks of wood on the sabbath. He knew that he was breaking the command to keep the sabbath day (see Exodus 20.8-11), but he did it anyway. Moses asked the Lord what they should do about this man and the Lord said he must be killed, **15.32-36**.

God also knew how quickly the people would forget Him and His commands, so He told them to put blue or violet thread into their clothes to remind them of the God of heaven, **15.37-41**.

In this chapter God makes provision for His children who do not know His commands or forget them, but He will not forgive those who know they are disobeying His commands, Hebrews 2.2,3.

Korah rebelled against God, chapter 16

2/14 The people of Israel had rebelled against God ad Kadesh-barnea and refused to enter the land of Canaan at that time. In chapter 33 there is a list of places they visited during their long journey in the desert. In chapters 15-19 we read some of the things that happened during these 38 years until they got back to Kadesh-barnea. The rebellion of Korah was the worst and most important of these events.

Korah belonged to the family of Kohath of the tribe of Levi. He had the privilege of helping to carry the furniture of the Tabernacle. Other Levites carried the boards and curtains of the Tabernacle, but it was a much greater honour to carry the furniture. Kohath was the grandfather of Korah and Moses and Aaron, so these three were cousins, Exodus 6.18-21.

Korah and two other men rebelled against Moses; these were Dathan and Abiram of the tribe of Reuben. Together Korah, Dathan and Abiram persuaded 250 of the leaders of the people to join them in their rebellion against Moses. They had seen God punish Miriam when she was jealous of Moses, chapter 12, but it seems that they had not learned the lesson that the Lord wanted to teach His people at that time. Perhaps Moses had asked God too soon to heal Miriam of her leprosy. If he had waited longer, men might have learned how serious Miriam's sin was. Now these 253 men told Moses and Aaron that they had no right to rule over God's people. They said that all the people of Israel were holy and that the Lord was among them, **16.1-3**. Moses answered them in verses 4 to 19, and God answered them in verses 20 to 40.

Moses fell on his face but he told the rebels that God would show His will on the next day. He told them to bring metal pots for burning incense to God as Nadab and Abihu had done, Leviticus 10.1. Moses said that he and Aaron did not think they were more important than the rest of the people. He also said that Korah and those with him were not as important as they thought they were, **16.4-7**. Then he spoke to Korah and all the Levites and said that they already had many special privileges, but now they wanted to be priests as well, **vs.8-11**.

2/15 Then Moses called Dathan and Abiram, but they refused to come to him, **16.12**. They said Moses had kept them from going into the fruitful land and now he wanted to kill them in the desert and rule over them, **vs.13,14**. Moses asked the Lord not to accept their offering and said that he had not done wrong to any of the people or taken anything that belonged to them, v.15. Moses told Korah and his men to come the next day before the Lord with incense in their pots. Aaron would do the same. Korah brought all the people together against Moses and Aaron before the Tabernacle, 16.16-19.

First God told Moses and Aaron to separate themselves from the crowd because He wanted to destroy the people in one minute. Moses and Aaron prayed for them, and said God should not be angry with the whole nation because only one man had sinned, 16.20-22. God agreed with their prayer and told the people to go away from Korah, Dathan and Abiram, vs.23,24.

2/16 Moses warned the people not to take anything that belonged to these men. Dathan and Abiram were not sorry for what they had done, but stood at the door of their tents together with their families, 16.25-27. Moses said that God would show who was right, Moses or Korah, Dathan and Abiram. They would die in a very unusual way. The ground would suddenly open up and they would fall alive into a deep hole and be killed. This would prove that God had chosen Moses to lead His people, vs.28-30.

At that very moment the earth shook. A great hole opened in the ground and the families of Korah, Dathan and Abiram fell into it with their tents and all that belonged to them. When the other people saw this they ran away because they were afraid that they too would be killed. The other 250 men were killed by fire from Jehovah, 16.31-35.

It is a terrible thing to fall into the hands of the living God.... for our God is indeed a destroying fire,
Hebrews 10.31; 12.29.

God told Eleazar the priest to take the copper pots of those who had been killed by the fire because these pots had been set apart for God. They were used to make a cover for the copper altar and reminded the people of Israel that they should not try to do the work of the priests, 16.36-40.

These 250 people had sinned against the Lord. They had also sinned against the people of Israel because they had tried to persuade them to rebel against Moses. God said that they died for their sin, v.38. Every sinner rebels against God and in the end he has to suffer for his actions.

2/17 The people had seen how God judged those who rebelled against Him, but they still felt sorry for the rebels. The next day they said Moses and Aaron had killed them unrighteously, **16.41**. The glory of the Lord appeared and He told Moses and Aaron again to separate themselves from the crowd so that He would be able to destroy the people in a minute. Moses and Aaron fell on their faces before the Lord, but Moses saw that God had already started to judge the people. Moses told Aaron to take a pot with fire and incense and to go quickly to the people, **16.42-46**.

Aaron always took a censer when he went into God's presence, Leviticus 16.12. Here he took a censer and asked the Lord not to kill any more of the people. An animal had died and had been burnt on the altar. This was the means by which the people's sin was forgiven; it was a picture of Christ, Romans 3.25.

Aaron ran among the people. He saw that a terrible disease was already spreading and some were dying. Aaron stood between the dead and the living and the disease did not spread any more, but 14,700 people had already died, **16.47-50**.

This chapter shows us how terrible it is to be jealous and to rebel against God. It also shows that the sin of one man can bring very much trouble into the lives of many people. Korah influenced Dathan and Abiram and these two men persuaded 250 of the leaders of Israel to follow them. Then these 250 men influenced the people of Israel to turn against Moses and Aaron. About 15,000 people died at this time. We can read a little about this sad event in Psalm 106.16-18 and Jude 11. God judged His people very severely at this time, but even so the children of Korah were not killed, Numbers 26.11; 1 Chronicles 6.22. In the old Hebrew Bible we see that ten of the psalms were written by or for the sons of Korah. Some of these are Psalm 42, 44, 45, 46, 47, 48, and 49.

No one in the Church today has the authority that Moses and Aaron had. In the New Testament some people refused to believe that God gave Paul authority to teach the way he did, 2 Timothy 1.15. At the present time also people rebel against God and refuse to believe His Word, the Bible. They say that God has spoken to men in other books and through other prophets as well. When they refuse the Word of God they refuse God Himself. In the New Testament we see that Christians should obey the elders of their church because God has given these elders the work of caring for the spiritual needs of the believers, Hebrews 13.17.

Aaron's stick sprouted leaves and flowers, chapter 17

2/18 The Lord wanted to show the people once again that He had chosen the tribe of Levi to serve Him. To prove this He commanded Moses to make a test. He said the leader of each tribe should bring a stick or rod and write his name on his rod. Aaron also brought a rod as the leader of the tribe of Levi. Moses put all these rods before the Lord in the Tabernacle. The next day everyone could see that Aaron's rod had sprouted leaves, flowers and nuts, **17.1-9**. God told Moses to keep Aaron's rod in the ark to remind the people that only the tribe of Levi should serve Him in the Tabernacle, **vs.10,11**; Hebrews 9.4. It would also be a warning to people of other tribes who might think of rebelling.

In chapter 16, 14,950 people died when God judged the people. In chapter 17 the Lord made Aaron's rod sprout leaves. This did not hurt anyone, but the people were more afraid than they were in 16.41. In chapter 16 they spoke against Moses. Now they made God's command sound worse than it really was; this shows they did not believe in His love, **17.12,13**. God had not said that a person would die if he came near the Tabernacle. This judgment was only for those who grumbled and rebelled against God. Many years before this Eve also made God's command sound worse than it was. She said that God told her and Adam not even to touch the tree in the middle of the garden of Eden, Genesis 3.3. God had said nothing about *touching* the tree; He had only commanded them not to *eat* any of the *fruit* of the tree, Genesis 2.17.

Aaron's rod grew leaves and fruit and is a picture of resurrection. God is able to bring life from dead wood; He is also able to raise dead men to life again. God raised the Lord Jesus Christ from death to show that He accepted Christ's sacrifice on the cross.

Jesus proved again and again that He is God, but still the teachers of the law asked for a sign to show that He was really God's Son. The Lord Jesus told them that they would be given only the sign of the prophet Jonah. What was this sign? Jonah was inside the large fish for three days and three nights before God made the fish vomit Jonah on the ground, Jonah 1.17; 2.10. When Jonah was inside the fish he was in a place of death. The Lord Jesus said He would be in the grave, the place for dead people, for three days and three nights. After that God would raise Him from death and bring Him out of the grave, Matthew 12.38-40. This sign is sufficient to prove to all men that God has chosen Christ to be the Saviour of the world.

The portion of the Levites, chapter 18

2/19 God had shown before that the Levites were specially near to Him. Now we read again about their work and their privileges.

Jehovah told Aaron that he and the Levites should look after the Tabernacle and that he and his sons should be the priests. God wanted the Levites to serve the priests, but told them they must not come near the things used for worship. They would die if they disobeyed this command, **18.1-7**.

God commanded that the priests should receive some of the offerings of the people of Israel, **18.8**. They also received part of the meal, sin and guilt offerings which were not burned on the altar. The priests were also given the best of the oil and the wine and the wheat, as well as the first-ripe fruit at harvest time, **vs.9-13**. In addition, all things that were set apart for God belonged to the priests, **v.14**, and the first born of clean animals also, **vs.15-18**. All these things belonged to the priests because God gave them to them, **v.19**.

2/20 The Lord also told Aaron that the Levites would not have any land of their own like the other tribes, but the Lord Himself belonged to them in a special way. The people of Israel had to give to the Lord one tenth of all they received, and this was for the Levites, **18.20-24**. Their work was to look after the Tabernacle because the people of Israel were not allowed to serve in it. But God provided well for His servants, the Levites, and they received more than the other tribes. However God knew that the people of Israel would not always bring in the tenth of what they received, Malachi 3.8.

The Lord wanted the Levites to offer Him one tenth of what they received, **18.25,26**. This was for Aaron, the priest, **vs.27-29**. We read that the Levites obeyed this command, Nehemiah 12.47. They could eat all the rest of the food they received, **vs.30-32**.

A Christian should give to the work of the Lord at least one tenth of what he receives. However we ourselves belong completely to the Lord, our bodies, our souls and our spirits. We should not keep for ourselves nine tenths of what we receive but give ourselves wholly to the Lord together with all that we have, 2 Corinthians 5.15. Read also Proverbs 3.9.

The priests received a better portion than the Levites, 18.12. In the same way those who worship the Lord have greater joy than those who only serve Him. The Lord Jesus praised Mary because she had chosen the right thing. She sat at Jesus' feet while Martha was busy serving, Luke 10.39-42.

Water for religious purification, chapter 19

2/21 Now the Lord gave Moses and Aaron another special law to be part of their worship. The people of Israel had to bring a young red cow which had no spot or defect, and which never had done any work or even had a yoke on its neck. Someone had to kill this animal in front of Eleazar the priest, **19.1-3**. The priest should sprinkle some of the blood before the Tabernacle and someone else should burn the animal. Usually the priest received the skin of the burnt offerings, Leviticus 7.8, but here everything was burned. This is a picture of Christ giving Himself even more completely to God. The priest also took some cedar wood, a plant called *hyssop*, and some bright red wool; he threw these things into the fire while the cow was burning, **vs.4-6**.

The people of Israel used hyssop to sprinkle the blood of the Passover, Exodus 12.22. They also had to use cedar wood and bright red wool and hyssop when a leper had been healed of his leprosy, Leviticus 14.4. Moses also used blood, water, bright red wool, and hyssop when he sprinkled the book of the law and the people of Israel, Exodus 24.8; Hebrews 9.19.

Those who helped in offering this sacrifice were unclean until evening. They were: 1) the person who burned the cow (perhaps this is the person who had killed it); 2) Eleazar the priest; 3) the man who gathered up the ashes afterwards, **19.7-10**. Also anyone who touched or used the water for religious cleansing was unclean until evening, v.21.

2/22 This water was used to cleanse anyone who had touched a dead body. When a man died in the tent, all the other people in the tent were unclean, also all who came into the tent; and everything in the tent, except covered pots. A person became unclean for seven days when he touched the dead body of a man who had been killed out in the open; or when he touched any dead person or a grave, **19.11-16**. An unclean person could not worship God until he became clean again.

How could he become clean? The people had to take some clean, running water from a spring and put some of the ashes of the young cow into it. A clean person had to dip some hyssop into this water and sprinkle it on the tent, pots or person on the third day and on the seventh day after he became unclean. On the seventh day the unclean person could wash himself and by evening he would be clean, **19.17-19**. Anyone who refused to do this would be put out of the nation of Israel, **vs.20-22**.

The ashes of the young cow could purify those who were religiously unclean. How much more is accomplished by the blood of Christ! His blood makes our consciences clean from useless works, so that we may serve the living God, Hebrews 9.13,14.

The perfect young cow had no spot or imperfections; it was a picture of the perfect Son of Man, the Lord Jesus Christ. The bright red colour speaks of suffering, and so reminds us of our Lord Jesus Christ.

This world is under the curse of death; we live in it and become unclean. It is very easy for those who are unclean to make others unclean, v.22. We need to have our feet washed daily with the water of the Word of God. Without this we cannot closely follow our Lord, John 13.8.

TEST YOURSELF - Numbers chapters 13-19

1. Why is Kadesh-barnea important?
2. Was it necessary for twelve men to walk through the whole land to find out if it was a good land?
3. How did the ten leaders make the people afraid?
4. Why were the people so angry with Caleb and Joshua?
5. What was the result of Moses' prayer?
6. How long did it take the men to look through the land? How long did God punish the rest of the nation for following the bad advice of ten men?
7. How does chapter 15, verses 1 to 13 show that God is gracious?
8. How can a believer become happier?
9. A man committed sin when he gathered sticks on the sabbath day. What sacrifice could he bring so that God would forgive him?
10. Why did Korah and other Levites try to rebel against Moses?
11. How did God show that He had chosen Aaron, not Korah?
12. How did the Levites get enough food for their families?
13. Why did the priest get the best of everything?
14. How could an unclean Israelite become clean again?
15. What can make a Christian unclean? How can he become clean again?

Turn to page 146 to check your answers.

KADESH TO CANAAN   4

2/23   Israel got back to Kadesh after wandering in the desert for 38 years. Kadesh was quite close to Canaan, but Israel had to fight against some of their enemies. Balaam and Balak wanted to curse Israel but God blessed them.

Back at Kadesh, chapter 20

We saw that the people of Israel had refused to go from Kadesh into the land of Canaan because they did not believe God would help them to overcome the people of the land, 13.26,31; 14.1-4. Since then 38 years had passed. The Bible tells us about only a few of the things that happened during this time. The most important was the rebellion of Korah, but the whole nation had the same attitude as Korah. Now most of the adults had died but the children had grown up during the journey through the desert.

Miriam, Moses' sister, was a prophetess. She had led the other women to praise the Lord when He saved the people of Israel from Egypt, Exodus 15.20. Miriam did not reach the land of Canaan either, but died at Kadesh, 20.1. It seemed as if the spirit of praise in Israel died with her, and the people were ready to grumble against the Lord once again.

You cannot praise the Lord
and grumble at the same time.

Perhaps Moses often obtained water from a rock, 1 Corinthians 10.4. Anyway now the people were thirsty again and could not wait for God to provide water for them. They began to argue with Moses and actually said they wished they had died together with those who had been judged by God, **20.2-5**; 16.49. Their fathers had said about the same thing 38 years before, Exodus 17.3. The children had not learned what the Lord tried to teach their fathers. The long journey through the desert had not changed their hearts.

Moses and Aaron did not argue with them, but went to the Tabernacle of Jehovah. The Lord told Moses to take his rod, but did not command him to strike the rock with it. He told Moses just to speak to the rock in order that the water might flow out, **20.6-8**. Moses was usually very humble, 12.3; this is true of all people who spend very much time in prayer to God. However this time he acted in a proud way. He spoke to the people (instead of to the rock, as God had told him to do) and called them rebels. Then he said to them, *Must WE get water out of this rock for you?* **vs.9-11**. But the worst thing he did was to strike the rock twice.

Plenty of water came out of the rock and the people and their cattle drank the water. But Moses had disobeyed God's command and acted proudly. God punished Moses and Aaron and said they could not lead Israel into the land of Canaan. In Deuteronomy 3.23-26 we see that Moses felt very badly about this.

Why was it so important for Moses to speak to the rock and not strike it? The Rock is often a name of God in Scripture, for example, Psalm 62.2, and here it is a picture of our Lord Jesus Christ, the Son of God. Moses' rod was a picture of the Law of God, because God gave Israel His Law through Moses. This Law says that every sinner must die but Christ died on the cross so we can live. He sets us free from the curse which the Law puts on us, and gives us life instead, Galatians 3.13.

Now years before this, God commanded Moses to strike the rock with his rod, Exodus 17.6. That was a picture of Christ dying on the cross and giving the water of life. He only had to die once; this one sacrifice was sufficient, Hebrews 9.28. So this time God told Moses only to speak to the rock. Instead he struck it the second time. This spoiled the picture: the Lord Jesus will never need to die again.

Before this the people had complained because they were thirsty and God provided water for them. The place where they complained was called Massah and Meribah, Exodus 17.7. Meribah means *arguing,* because the people argued there with Jehovah. The Lord gave them what they needed but showed them that He is holy, **20.13**.

2/24 After this Moses asked the king of Edom to help them. He appealed to him by calling God's people "your brother Israel." The Edomites were the descendants of Esau, and Jacob and Esau were brothers. Moses told the king of Edom how the people of Israel had been slaves in Egypt. He thought this would make the king feel sorry for them. Then he asked the king to allow them to go through his country. He promised that all the people would stay on the road, and that they would not take any food growing in the fields. They would pay for any water that they might drink, **20.14-17**. The king of Edom refused to help them in any way and his army came out ready to fight with them. So the people of Israel went into the desert again, **vs.18-21**.

We should not ask nor expect the people of the world to help us in the work of the Lord, Galatians 6.14. The Lord had not told Moses to ask the Edomites if Israel could pass through their land. How then could Moses know that the people would get the manna each day or that the cloud would go before them as they passed through the land of Edom?

Moses' troubles were not yet over. At the beginning of this chapter we read about the death of Miriam and now we read that Aaron died. In between Moses had disobeyed the Lord when he struck the rock twice and the Edomites refused to help the people of Israel. Now Moses, Aaron and Eleazar climbed Mount Hor together. Moses put Aaron's clothes on Eleazar, and Aaron died on top of the mountain. He was 123 years old when he died and had been travelling through the desert for over 39 years, 33.38,39. The people of Israel mourned for him for 30 days, **20.22-29**.

Eleazar became high priest in the place of Aaron, and after him many others of his descendants. These high priests were quite different from our Great High Priest who died and rose again from death. The Lord Jesus Christ is High Priest for ever and He will not die and pass His work as priest on to someone else. He lives for ever to plead with God for His people, Hebrews 7.23-25.

Moses and Aaron both had part in striking the rock the second time. This would mean that the one sacrifice of Christ was not enough. God was angry and did not allow Moses and

Aaron to lead the people into the land of Canaan. Today the Roman Catholic Church teaches that Christ is sacrificed again every time the priests hold the Mass. People who believe this can never be sure that God has forgiven their sins, Hebrews 10.11-14.

Journeys and war, chapter 21

2/25 A king of the land of Canaan wanted to make sure that the Israelites would not come into his country. He and his soldiers went to fight with them and made some of them his prisoners. However the Israelites believed what God had promised them in Exodus 23.27,31, and God helped them to overcome these enemies and destroy their cities, **21.1-3**.

In spite of this victory the people felt very badly because they had to travel all the way around the land of Edom. Again they complained against the Lord and against Moses. They said they did not have any bread or water. Of course they had the manna which God provided for them day by day, but they were tired of it, **21.4,5**.

This time God punished them by sending poisonous snakes among them. These snakes bit the people and many of them died, **21.6**. Then the people came to Moses and confessed that they had sinned. They asked Moses to pray that God would take the snakes away. God is always gracious and He did even more than what they asked for. He provided a way by which those already bitten could be healed. Moses made a snake of brass and put it on a pole. Every Israelite who had been bitten by a snake was healed when he believed the promise of God and looked at the brass snake on the pole, **vs.7-9**.

The brass snake was a picture of our Lord Jesus Christ who was lifted up on the cross, John 3.14. The snake is a picture of sin and death. It was made of brass which speaks of judgment. The only way we can be saved is to look to Another. The Lord Jesus Christ took our place as sinners and died for us.

Many times God in His grace does much more than what men ask Him for. For example, the younger son asked his

2/26   father to allow him to be one of his servants, but his father received him again as his son, Luke 15.19-24.

Next the people of Israel travelled from Oboth to Pisgah, **21.10-20.** The Israelites were coming closer to the land of Canaan, where many people lived in towns. We see that God did not provide everything for them by miracles as He had done in the desert. When they needed water the leaders dug a well. Through this well the Lord provided more than enough water for the people and they praised Him with the song in verses 17 and 18.

After this we read about the first of Israel's victories as they fought to get the whole land of Canaan. Sihon was the king of the Amorites. The people of Israel sent messengers to him to ask him to allow them to pass through his land. They promised not to spoil his fields or drink his water, but Sihon refused to give them permission. Instead he and his men came to fight with them. The Israelites defeated them in the battle and took the land of the Amorites, **21.21-25.** This encouraged the people of Israel because Sihon was a great soldier. Before this battle he had overcome the king of Moab and taken his land, **v.26.** Someone had made up a song about how Sihon defeated the king of Moab, **vs.27-30.**

2/27   Then Og, the king of Bashan, came to fight with Israel. The Lord encouraged Israel to go and fight with him and his people. They defeated the king of Bashan and occupied his land also, **21.31-35.** Sihon and Og both lived on the east side of the Jordan River.

These victories were very important at that time and gave the people of Israel courage to fight with other enemies later on. The men of Jericho began to be afraid when they heard how the people of Israel had overcome Sihon and Og, Joshua 2.10. People still remembered these victories many years later, Psalm 135.10,11; 136.18-20.

In the same way the Lord gives us the victory in our spiritual lives, and encourages us to go on, trusting Him and expecting Him to do great things in us and through us.

Balaam, chapters 22-25

2/28   We should be especially watchful whenever God has given us a victory because at that time Satan will attack us and try to make us sin. The next four chapters tell the story of Balaam. Balaam could not curse the people of God, but succeeded by a trick. He led them into sin and God had to punish them.

Balak called Balaam, chapter 22

The people of Israel approached the land of Canaan and came to the country of Balak, king of Moab. Balak knew how powerful the people of Israel were. He was afraid of them and tried to resist them by means of his religion. He joined with the elders of the land of Midian and sent some of them with a message to Balaam, the son of Beor. Balaam was a prophet of God, but he said what God told him, only because God made him say it, not because he really loved the Lord, **22.1-6**.

The elders of Moab and Midian came to ask Balaam to curse the people of Israel. They brought money to give to him if he would agree to do so. Balaam told them to wait until the next morning so that he could ask God to show him what he should do. God told him that He had already blessed Israel, and that Balaam would not be able to curse them. Balaam was very sorry about this and told the messengers that God would not allow him to go with them, **22.7-13**.

Balak did not accept Balaam's answer and sent another committee to him, men who were more important than the first. These men promised Balaam that he would receive great honour if he would obey the king. Balaam repeated that he could say only what the Lord told him to say, no matter how much silver and gold Balak gave him. However he said he would ask the Lord again about this matter. God knew the thoughts in Balaam's heart and allowed him to go this time, **22.14-21**.

2/29 Still God was angry with Balaam and sent an angel to stand in his path. Balaam was riding on a donkey to go to Balak. The donkey saw the angel with a sword in his hand and turned off the road. Balaam could not see the angel and so he beat the donkey. Then the angel appeared again where the path was very narrow between two fences. The donkey tried to get out of the angel's way and crushed Balaam's foot against the fence. Balaam became angry and beat the donkey again. The third time the angel appeared and the donkey fell down under Balaam and Balaam beat her even more. This time the Lord made the donkey speak, **22.22-30.** At last the Lord also opened Balaam's eyes and Balaam saw the angel and was very frightened. The angel told Balaam that his journey did not please God. Balaam offered to go back, but showed that he really wanted to go on, so the angel allowed him to continue his journey, **vs.31-35.**

At last Balaam and Balak met. Balaam repeated that he could say only what God told him to say, **22.36-41.**

Balaam's First Prophecy, 23.1-12

2/30 Balak took Balaam to a high place where his people worshipped their god Baal. From there he wanted Balaam to see the camp of Israel in the distance. Balaam told the king to build seven altars at that place and offer on each of them a bull and a ram, **23.1,2.** Then Balaam went off by himself and the Lord put some words in his mouth, **vs.3-6.** He returned to Balak and told him the prophecy which the Lord had given him. Balak was very angry when he heard it because he said God had blessed Israel and would not curse them at all. Balaam still seemed to be sorry that he could say only what the Lord told him to say, **vs.11,12.**

Balaam's Second Prophecy, 23.13-25

3/1 Balak thought he would try again to get Balaam to curse Israel. This time he took the prophet to another place where he could see only a part of the camp of Israel. Again Balak built seven altars and offered a bull and a ram on each one. Then Balaam went to meet the Lord again, and returned with a message. He told Balak that God cannot change or lie. He did not see sin in Israel and no one could prophesy evil about them. The king told Balaam that he should neither curse the people, nor bless them.

Balaam's Third Prophecy, 23.26 - 24.9

Balaam insisted that he could only say what the Lord told him to say, but both he and Balak were willing to try a third time. This time they went to the top of Mount Peor, built more altars and brought offerings as before, **23.26-30.** Balaam did not go to ask the Lord for His message, but the Spirit of God came on him anyway, **24.1,2.** He told about the order and beauty of the camp of Israel and how the nation and her king would be victorious and become great, **vs.3-8.** Finally he repeated the promise God had given to Abraham, *Blessed be they that bless you, and they that curse you be accursed,* **v.9,** Genesis 12.3.

Balaam's Fourth Prophecy, 24.10-25

3/3 Balak had now killed 42 animals, but the prophet had only blessed his enemies. So the king sent Balaam back to his own country without giving him a gift, **24.10,11.** Before Balaam left he prophesied again and said that the people of Israel would overcome the Edomites and the Moabites. A king would arise in Israel who would rule over the neighbouring countries. The Amalekites and the Kenites would be completely destroyed, **vs.12-24.** After this Balaam and Balak separated, **v.25.**

Balaam's success, chapter 25

God could speak through prophets who were not Israelites and sometimes He did so. Balaam prayed to God and could speak for God, but he did it because he wanted money. We find his name three times in the New Testament. We read about the way of Balaam, 2 Peter 2.15; the error of Balaam, Jude 11; and the teaching of Balaam, Revelation 2.14. The way of Balaam was to love the money he could get for doing wrong. The error of Balaam was to use the name of Jehovah while practising false religion in order to get money. The teaching of Balaam was to show Balak how he could hurt Israel by leading them into sin. In Numbers 25 we read only that the people of Israel sinned with Moabitish women and brought sacrifices to worship their idols. In Revelation 2.14 we see that Balaam taught Balak how he could make the people of Israel sin against the Lord.

Balaam was a false prophet and was destroyed together with the kings of Midian, Numbers 31.8. He could not curse the people of Israel because God had blessed them, but he loved money. This made him show Balak how he could bring God's judgment on the people. Today many people do not really believe in Christ nor love God. They continue to use the name of Christian because they want money. Peter and Jude tell us what will happen in the last days, but Revelation 2 shows that this has been going on for hundreds of years among those who call themselves Christians.

3/4 The Lord became angry with Israel when they committed adultery with the Moabitish women and worshipped their idols. Of course God had seen the sins of Israel before this. They were just finishing 40 years of punishment for their sins, 14.34, but this was a family matter between God and His children. He could say to their enemies that He had not seen sin in the descendants of Jacob, 23.21.

God had protected His people and refused to curse them, but even so they had to be punished when they fell into sin. The men who had done these things were to be killed, **25.1-5**. Some people were really sorry for what they had done, but one man actually brought a Midianite woman into his tent in front of Moses and the people, **v.6**. Phinehas, Aaron's grandson, went and killed both the man and the woman with a spear. This stopped the terrible disease which God had sent among the people. However 24,000 people had already died, **vs.7-9**. The Lord honoured Phinehas and promised him that he would be the priest and his sons would serve as priests as long as that age continued, **vs.10-15**. God told Israel to fight with the Midianites, **25.16-18**. In 31.1-12 we see that they obeyed this command.

Descendants of Aaron will serve as priests in the Temple when Christ will reign as King over this earth for 1000 years, Ezekiel 44.15; 1 Chronicles 6.3,8. At the present time the Lord Jesus Christ has taken the place of the descendants of Aaron and He is our Great High Priest, Hebrews 4.14; 7.24.

All these things show us very wonderfully that God is faithful and gracious and righteous. When Satan tries to accuse God's people, the Lord blesses and justifies them, Romans 8.33,34. God cannot close His eyes to the sins of His people, Hebrews 12.6, but He will honour those who are faithful to Him, as Phinehas was.

TEST YOURSELF - Numbers chapters 20-25

1. Why was God angry when Moses struck the rock the second time?
2. Name two people who died in Numbers 20.
3. How do we know that the brass serpent is a picture of our Lord Jesus Christ?
4. In the desert God provided water by a miracle but how did Israel get water when they came near the land of Canaan?
5. Why were the victories over Sihon and Og very important?
6. Why was Balak afraid?
7. What did Balak plan to do?
8. Why did Balaam refuse to do what Balak wanted?
9. Why did Balak refuse to pay Balaam?
10. What does the New Testament say about Balaam?
11. How did Balaam succeed in hurting the people of Israel?
12. How did God punish Israel?

Turn to page 147 to check your answers.

Commands for Israel in the Land of Canaan

5

3/5 In this lesson we will study chapters 26 to 36 and see that Moses again counted the people of Israel. The Lord named Joshua to be the leader of Israel and commanded the people to punish Midian. Moses gave land to two and a half tribes on the west side of the Jordan River. We will also see that the Lord gave instructions about women, about the offerings, and about the land of Canaan. Let us ask the Lord to help us understand these chapters in His Word.

The people were counted a second time, chapter 26

The fourth book of Moses is called Numbers because all the people of Israel were counted on two different occasions. They were counted at the beginning of their journey through the desert and at the end of it. We read about the first counting in chapter 1.

3/6 Now God commanded Moses and Eleazar, the priest, to count the men who were twenty years old or more and healthy enough to be soldiers, **26.2; 1.3**. In 26.5-51 the tribes are listed in almost the same order as in chapter 1. Six of the tribes had a few more men than at the beginning of the journey, but the total of all Israel was about 2,000 men less than before.

Chapter 1	Tribe	Chapter 26
46,000	Reuben	43,730
59,300	Simeon	22,200
45,650	Gad	40,500
74,600	Judah	76,500
54,400	Issachar	64,300
57,400	Zebulun	60,500
32,200	Manasseh	52,700
40,500	Ephraim	32,500

56

Chapter 1	Tribe	Chapter 26
35,400	Benjamin	45,600
62,700	Dan	64,400
41,500	Asher	53,400
53,400	Naphthali	45,400
603,550		601,730

In chapter 26 we also have the names of the families of the different tribes. More details and some changes are found in the first few chapters of 1 Chronicles.

3/7 Jehovah told Moses how much land each tribe should receive when they entered Canaan, 26.52-56. The larger tribes would get more land than the smaller tribes. However He wanted them to do everything by drawing lots. Before the Bible was completely written people often used this method to find out the Lord's will in any problem.

Then we read the names of the heads of the families of Levi, also the number of boys and men one month old and more, 26.57-62. There were 23,000 of these; this was 1,000 more than at the beginning of the journey, 3.39.

We see that God gave the greatest privileges to the smallest tribe. He does the same today for those people who do not get much honour from the people of the world, 1 Corinthians 1.27.

In this chapter we are reminded of two different occasions when God judged those who rebelled against Him. In verses 9 and 10 we read of the death of Dathan and Abiram and Korah and his followers, chapter 16. Verse 61 tells of the death of Nadab and Abihu who brought their own burning incense to Jehovah, Leviticus 10.1-3. These men were representatives of the whole nation which rebelled at Kadesh-barnea. God had said that none of the adults would enter the land except Caleb and Joshua, 14.29-33. Now they were in the plains of Moab near the river Jordan and all the adults who had left Egypt had died in the desert, 26.63-65.

These things teach us two things: God's mercy is very great for those who fear Him, but His righteousness should make us afraid to do anything that is not pleasing to Him. You will be very sorry later on if you turn back from following the Lord.

Women can own property, 27.1-11

3/8 Zelophehad was a man of the tribe of Manasseh, 26.33. He had five daughters, but no sons. These five daughters came to Moses to ask for a share of the land with the other members of the tribe, 27.1-4. Moses asked Jehovah about this problem and the Lord made a rule that a man's property should go to his daughter if he had no son when he died. If he had neither son nor daughter, his brothers would get the property or his nearest relative, **vs.5-11**.

Joshua is appointed to take Moses' place, 27.12-23

3/9 Then the Lord commanded Moses to climb Mount Abarim so he could have a look at the land of Canaan before he died. Moses could not enter the land because he had rebelled against the Lord at Meribah, **27.12-14**.

Moses accepted this punishment, but asked the Lord to raise up a man who would act as a shepherd for the people of Israel, **27.15-17**. The Lord chose Joshua, the son of Nun, for this work. The Holy Spirit had come on him, **v.18**, and God told Moses to give him some of his own authority in front of all the people, **vs.19,20**. The Lord would guide Joshua by means of the *Urim,* which was part of the breast plate of the high priest, Exodus 28.30. If Joshua had a special problem, he could tell Eleazar, the high priest, about it. Eleazar would then ask God to reveal His will about the matter through the Urim, **v.21**. Moses did what the Lord commanded, **vs.22,23**.

After our Saviour died on the cross He sent the Holy Spirit to live in the heart of each believer, to guide him and reveal God's will to him, John 16.7,13.

Numbers 27-29 59

Sacrifices to be offered at certain times of the year, chapters 28, 29.

3/10 The people of Israel were sorry to hear that Moses was going to die. At this very time God told them again about the different sacrifices which made it possible for them to come to Him and worship. These sacrifices reminded God of the death of Christ. Some of the laws in this chapter had already been given in Leviticus 23. Others added more details to the instructions which God had given before.

The Lord wanted them to bring Him a burnt offering every day, a sheep in the morning and a sheep in the evening, **28.1-8**. They also had to bring a meal offering and a drink offering. The meal offering was four pints of flour mixed with 1 1/2 pints of oil and the drink offering was 1 1/2 pints of wine, Exodus 29.38-42. On the sabbath day the Lord wanted them to offer four sheep together with the meal and drink offerings, **vs.9,10**.

On the first day of each month they were to offer two bulls, a ram, and seven young sheep for a burnt offering, together with their meal, oil, and wine offerings. They also had to bring a goat for a sin offering, **28.11-15**.

3/11 Then the Lord gave instructions again about the six feasts which the people should keep each year. The Feast of Unleavened Bread followed the Feast of the Passover. For the Feast of Unleavened Bread they brought the same offerings as they did on the first day of every month, **28.16-25**. On the day of Firstfruits they brought the same offering and the meal and drink offerings, **vs.26-31**.

3/12 Most of the feasts were in the first month or the seventh month. The Feast of Trumpets was on the first day of the seventh month, **29.1-6**. At this feast they offered the usual special burnt offerings to be offered on the first day of the month, and in addition a special burnt offering of one bull (not two), one ram and seven sheep with the meal and drink offerings, and a goat for a sin offering. On the day of Atonement these offerings were all offered again in addition to the special sin offering, **vs.7-11**; Leviticus 16.

3/13 Finally the Feast of Tabernacles began on the fifteenth day and lasted for one week, **29.12-38**. For seven days they offered every day two rams and 14 sheep and a goat for a sin offering with the meal and drink offerings. In addition they offered a number of bulls, thirteen the first day, twelve the second, eleven on the third, one less each day, until on the seventh day they offered only seven bulls. On the eighth day they offered one bull, one ram, seven sheep and a goat for a sin offering, as on the first day and the tenth day of the month.

3/14 God commanded the whole nation to offer these sacrifices, but any individual could bring more offerings to the Lord of his own free will for special purposes, **29.39,40**.

What does all this mean to us today? We can say that all the different animal sacrifices are pictures of our Lord Jesus Christ in various ways. See *Studies in Exodus and Leviticus,* on Leviticus 1-7. God the Father is always glad to be reminded of Christ's perfections and so are those who love the Lord Jesus.

Why did the people offer fewer bulls each day of the Feast of Tabernacles? This feast speaks of the Millennium when Christ will rule over the earth for 1000 years. It may be that during that time believers will think less and less of Christ.

This can also happen in the life of an individual believer or in an assembly today. For example at Ephesus the saints did not always love the Lord as much as they did at the beginning, Revelation 2.4. How can we keep our love for Christ from growing less? We should spend time every day studying and thinking about the Word of God, and in prayer and fellowship with the Lord Himself.

Vows of women, chapter 30

3/15 A man could promise with a vow to do something for the Lord or give something to Him and he had to fulfil his vow. A woman was under the authority of her father. She could make a vow to the Lord, but her father could cancel it and she would not have to fulfil it. However her father must do this *immediately,* or she would have to fulfil her vow, **30.1-5**.

3/16 A married woman was under the authority of her husband. He could cancel her vow on the same day he heard about it. In this case the woman was not guilty before the Lord if she did not fulfil the vow. However if her husband did not cancel her vow right away, she had to fulfil her promise, **30.6-16**. A widow or divorced woman always had to fulfil any vow she made to the Lord, v.9.

The woman in Israel had more rights than women of other nations, but still she was under God's law. The New Testament teaches us clearly about the woman's place in the Church at the present time. See 1 Corinthians 11.5-16; 14.34,35; 1 Timothy 2.11-14. God had very good reasons for giving these instructions. The Christian woman who really loves the Lord will not rebel against them and insist on her "rights", but will try to please her wonderful Saviour in every way she can.

The Midianites are punished, 31.1-20

3/17 God did not allow Balaam to curse the people of Israel, chapters 22-25, so Balaam showed the king of the Midianites that he could harm the Israelites by leading them into sin, Revelation 2.14. At that time the Lord had told Israel to make the Midianites suffer and to strike them down, 25.16-18. Now the Lord told them to revenge themselves on the Midianites and pay them back for the evil they had done to them, **31.1,2**.

Today a Christian should never take revenge, Romans 12.19, but God will certainly punish those who hurt His people, Jude 14,15.

Phinehas, the priest, led 12,000 men to fight against the Midianites. They killed all the men as well as the five kings of Midian. Balaam knew that God would bless Israel, but he still chose to be with their enemies and so he was killed with them, **31.3-8**.

3/18 The Israelite soldiers wanted to keep the Midianite women and children, but Moses understood that this would be wrong also. He allowed them to keep only the young, unmarried girls; all the others were killed, **31.9-18**. The soldiers had to stay outside the camp for seven days, then they could return, **vs.19,20**.

Things taken from the enemy after the battle, 31.21-54

The soldiers had taken many valuable things after the battle, some made of metal, some made of wood or other material. All these things were unclean and Eleazar told the soldiers how to make them clean. They could use fire to make the metal things clean but of course fire would destroy other material. They should take some of the water with ashes in it, 19.9, and use it to make everything clean, 31.21-23.

At the Judgment Seat of Christ the work of all believers will be tested with fire, 2 Corinthians 5.10; 1 Corinthians 3.11-15. Gold, silver and precious stones speak of our good works which were done to please and glorify the Lord. These will not be burned but the fire will destroy everything else. Many believers will learn at that time that they have wasted most of their lives.

3/19 The people who stayed at home received the same as the soldiers who went to the battle: sheep, cattle, donkeys and slave girls which the soldiers had brought back from the battle, **31.25-27.** The soldiers had to give one part out of every 500 to the Lord, and the other people one part out of every 50. This portion was for Eleazar, the priest, **vs.28-47.**

3/20 Then the officers and captains counted their men and found that not one had been killed in the war. They therefore brought another gift of gold to the Lord of their own free will. This weighed 16,750 shekels. Moses and Eleazar brought this gold into the Tabernacle, **31.48-54.**

We see that the officers gave to the Lord more than what they had been commanded to give. In the Old Testament God told His people to give to Him one tenth of all they received, but they could bring other gifts as well if they wished. Christians are no longer under law, but are under grace. We should understand that everything we receive and have belongs to the Lord, not only one tenth of it. It is sad that many Christians give the Lord only one tenth, and many do not even give Him that much.

The request of Reuben and Gad, chapter 32

3/21 In Old Testament times a rich person was one whom God had blessed. The people of the tribes of Reuben and Gad had plenty of sheep and cattle. However they did not seem to understand that God had given them these riches and that He would also be able to take care of them. They noticed that the land was good for cattle, so they said they wanted to live on the east side of the river Jordan, not in the land of Canaan, **32.1-5**.

Moses tried to show them that this would not be right at all. He reminded them how angry the Lord was when the people of Israel refused to enter the land of Canaan the first time they came to Kadesh-barnea. Now these two tribes did not want to go into the land. The rest of the people would lose courage and refuse to fight for the land God had given them, **32.6-15**.

3/22 The people of Reuben and Gad offered to go across the Jordan and fight against the enemy together with the other tribes. They would first prepare a place for their families and would return to them later, **32.16-19**. This was a little better and Moses accepted their suggestion, **vs.20-24**. He insisted that all the soldiers must go over Jordan and remain there until the Israelites had overcome the people of the land, vs.21,22. The people of Reuben and Gad repeated that they would do this, **vs.25-27**.

3/23 Then Moses called Eleazar and Joshua and the leaders of the people. He told them that they should give the land of Gilead to Reuben and Gad if they fulfilled their promise, **32.28-30**. The people of Reuben and Gad repeated that they would do what they had said they would do, **vs.31,32**.

God had already told Moses that the people should cast lots for the land so that it would be divided according to *God's* will and not their own, 26.55. It seems that Moses had forgotten this command. Now half of the tribe of Manasseh joined the people of Reuben and Gad, **32.33**. They built a number of cities for their families while the rest of the people of Israel had to wait for them. They gave some of these cities new names and called some by the name of the leader of the tribe, as Jair and Nobah, **vs.34-42**.

The tribes of Reuben and Gad and the half tribe of Manasseh are a picture of people who want to have some connection with the people of God and at the same time enjoy the pleasures of this world. Since they live in the world, they must of course also share the judgments of the world. These two and a half tribes partly fulfilled their promise and sent at least some of their soldiers to help Israel on the western side of the Jordan. However they were not always a blessing to the other tribes. Later God had to punish Israel because of their disobedience. He allowed Gentile kings to take the people of Israel to their own land as prisoners. At that time these two and a half tribes were the first ones who were taken away, 1 Chronicles 5.26.

Don't you know that to be the world's friend means to be God's enemy? Whoever wants to be the world's friend makes himself God's enemy, James 4.4.

Journeys from Egypt to Jordan, chapter 33

3/24   The people of Israel wandered in the desert for 38 years after they refused to enter the land of Canaan. Now God commanded Moses to write down the names of all the places where they had stopped during those years, **33.1,2**. Most of these places are not mentioned in Exodus or Numbers. Many of them are not referred to anywhere else in the Bible and we do not know today just where they were located.

The people of Israel left Egypt on the fifteenth day of the first month of the first year, **33.3**. In verses **5-15** we see the names of the places where they stopped on their way to Mount Sinai. In Exodus chapters 13-15 we read about their journey to the Red Sea and on to Elim. In Numbers 33.10 we see that they returned again to the Red Sea and then went on to Sinai, v.15.

3/25   The book of Numbers tells us some of the things which took place on the journey from Sinai to Kadesh-barnea, **33.16,17**, chapters 10,12. Kadesh-barnea is called Hazeroth in 33.17. See 12.16 and 13.26.

Then we see that they stopped at many places while they wandered in the desert before they came back to Kadesh, **33.18-36**. This time they were ready to go in and occupy the land which the Lord had given them and they moved on to Mount Hor on the border of the land of Edom, v.37. Aaron was 123 years old when he died, **33.38,39**. We already read about his death in 20.22-29. The Canaanites mentioned in **verse 40** were destroyed by the people of Israel, 21.3.

/26 Israel travelled on to the plains of Jordan opposite Jericho, **33.41-49**. In this chapter we do not read how the people of Israel disobeyed the Lord at Kadesh-barnea. God must punish those who sin, but if they repent, He will not mention their sin again. For this reason we do not read in the New Testament about the sins of God's people who lived in Old Testament times. God will never again remember the sins of those who believe in His Son, the Lord Jesus Christ, Hebrews 8.12.

/27 Now on the shore of the Jordan the people of Israel heard the Lord's command to drive out the people of the land before them, to destroy their idols, and to divide the land among themselves by drawing lots. If they allowed the Canaanites to live, they would always trouble Israel and bother them, **33.50-56**.

The Canaanites make us think of sinful habits of a person before he believed in Christ. Now he is a Christian, and he must overcome these bad habits with the Lord's help. If he does not do this, they will continually drag him into sin and spoil his fellowship with the Lord.

Borders of the land of Canaan, chapter 34

/28 So the Lord commanded Israel to drive the Canaanites out of their land, and then He told them where the borders of the promised land would be, **34.1-15**. We do not know today where many of these places were. However it is clear that the Mediterranean Sea was the western border, v.6, and the river Jordan was the eastern border, v.12. Kadesh-barnea was at the southern end of the land, v.4, and Mount Hor and Lebo-hamath at the northern end, vs.7,8. You can see these places on a map of Palestine. Moses knew that the two and a half tribes would occupy the land on the east side of Jordan, vs.14,15, but this was not really part of the land which the Lord had promised.

The people of Israel did not fully occupy this land until the time of King Solomon. This is a picture of many Christians today who enjoy only a part of all the blessings which they have in Christ.

3/29 This land had to be divided among the 9½ tribes. The Lord chose twelve men to look after this work. Eleazar the priest was one of the twelve, also Joshua, the son of Nun. The others were leaders of the nine tribes and of the half tribe of Manasseh as well, **34.16-29.** In Joshua chapters 15 to 19 we can read how this was done.

Cities of refuge, chapter 35

3/30 The tribe of Levi did not receive part of the land with the other tribes. God commanded the other tribes to give 48 of their own cities for the Levites to live in together with some land around these cities, **35.1-8.** The people obeyed this command in Joshua 21. When Israel lived in the land, the Levites did not have to carry the Tabernacle any more, but they had other work to do in it. They received gifts from the other tribes and did not have to make farms for themselves.

4/1 Six of the 48 cities of the Levites were also *cities of refuge.* If an Israelite accidentally killed someone he could run away from the angry relatives to one of these six cities. In the city of refuge he was safe and no one could hurt him. Three of these cities were on the east side of Jordan and three on the west side. These cities would not protect someone who hated another person and killed him. The relative of the dead person could kill the murderer as soon as he caught him. This was the law of God, **35.9-21**; Genesis 9.6; Exodus 21.12-14; Leviticus 24.17.

4/2 When anyone escaped to the city of refuge the people of the city had to judge if this person had killed the other one purposely or not. He would be protected in the city of refuge only if he had killed the other person accidentally without hating him, and he had to stay inside the city until the high priest died, **35.22-25.** If he left the city, the dead person's relatives could kill him, **vs.26-29.**

We see here a picture of the nation of Israel which committed murder when they asked Pilate to crucify the Lord Jesus Christ. They did not know what they were doing because they did not understand who He was. The nation of Israel was driven away and could not live in their own land, but was still protected by God. After the Church Age Israel will be blessed again as a nation, more than ever before.

4/3 After these instructions the Lord commanded Israel to punish all murderers, **35.30-34**. No one could be put to death unless at least two witnesses saw him commit murder, v.30. The murderer could not save himself by paying money and the person who had accidentally killed someone could not pay money in order to leave the city of refuge, vs.31,32. God would judge the nation for anyone who was killed, vs.33,34. All these laws do not apply to individual persons today, but many nations have based their laws on the laws of Israel. In many countries murderers do not have to die. This shows how men are always changing God's law.

More about the daughters of Zelophehad, chapter 36

/4 We have already read about the daughters of Zelophehad in 27.1-11. The Lord had promised them that they should receive the land of their father. Now the leaders of the family of Gilead asked what would happen to this land if these daughters married men from other tribes, **36.1-4**. They were afraid that part of their land would then go to another tribe. They knew that every man's land would come back to him in the fiftieth year, the year of jubile, Leviticus 25.10,28, but they were afraid that the land of Zelophehad would not be returned to the tribe of Manasseh.

Moses agreed that the daughters of Zelophehad could marry anyone they wished as long as their husbands were of the tribe of Manasseh. This became a rule for all Israel, **36.5-9**. The daughters of Zelophehad obeyed it and married husbands of their own tribe, **vs.10-12**. The last verse (36.13) refers to the last part of the book, chapters 22-36, especially chapters 27-30 and 34-36.

The leaders of Gilead had a real desire to keep the land which God had given them. They also remembered the law of the year of Jubilee although we never read that the people of Israel obeyed it. However they had chosen to live on the east side of Jordan together with the tribes of Reuben and Gad. They were not following the Lord completely, and they could not trust Him to take care of their land for them; they wanted to have everything arranged in advance.

Some Christians do not live truly separated from the world; they always find it difficult to trust the Lord. For this reason Abraham went down to Egypt and was afraid the Egyptians would kill him because of his wife, Genesis 12.11-13. Saul could not trust the Lord when the Philistines came to fight with him, so he asked a witch what he should do, 1 Samuel 28. When we are walking with the Lord we can trust Him fully.

I will fear no evil, for you are with me,
Psalm 23.4.

TEST YOURSELF - Numbers chapters 26-36

1. Did the number of people increase while they were travelling 38 years through the desert?
2. What did Zelophehad's daughters ask for?
3. Who chose Joshua to lead the people of Israel?
4. How many sheep were offered every day to Jehovah?
   How many sheep were offered every sabbath day?
   How many sheep were offered on the first day of each month?
5. What do these animal sacrifices speak about?
6. Why did a man have the right to cancel his wife's promise to give something to the Lord?
7. Why did God tell Israel to avenge themselves on the people of Midian?
8. How did the soldiers make clean the things they had taken in the battle?
9. Why did Reuben and Gad want to remain outside the land of Canaan?

10. What command did Moses forget when he gave land to Reuben and Gad?
11. What does chapter 33 tell us?
12. Where are the places which are listed in chapter 34?
13. Why did God set apart six cities, as cities of refuge?
14. Why did Moses command the daughters of Zelophehad to marry someone in their own tribe?

Turn to page 147 to check your answers.

The Teaching of Numbers 6

Take a piece of paper about as big as this whole page and cover up everything on this page except what you are reading just now. You can move the paper down a little at a time so you can read more. Each paragraph or section of the page has a line under it. A paragraph with a line under it is called a frame. You should read only one frame at a time, and keep the rest of the page covered with the piece of paper. Each frame will tell you a little more.

Each frame also has a question or a space at the end. This is to see if you have understood the main teaching of the frame. Try to answer the question or write the missing word in the empty space. If you cannot answer the question, read the frame again. When you think you know the right answer, move the paper down so you can see the next frame. Before you read anything in the next frame, look first at the **right** side of the frame. This gives the correct answer to the question in the first frame. If you had the right answer, this shows that you have understood the most important part of the first frame. You are now ready to go on to read everything in the **second** frame. IF you did not get the right answer, you are not ready to go on. You should read the first frame again and really try to understand it. When you understand the first frame then you can go on to the second frame. Read this frame carefully and answer the question at the end. Then go on to the third frame and all the others, one by one.

4/5 1. In the book of Numbers we learn that God spoke to Moses many times, and the Lord gave him many commands. We can say that God led Moses to write this book and told him what to say. The book of Numbers is *inspired;* this is also true of the 66 books of the whole Bible. The Lord Jesus knew that the book of Numbers is true, John 3.14. The book of Numbers is _____ and so are the other 65 books of the Bible.

---

2. Numbers also teaches us a great deal about God. The   *1. inspired*
great lesson of the Old Testament is that God is righteous and
holy, and Numbers teaches this also. God showed that He is righteous when He punished Miriam at once because she spoke against Moses, 12.10. God punished the whole nation because they refused to enter the land of Canaan, and especially the men who had given a false report, 14.29,37. What does this show about God? _____

The Teaching of Numbers

3. Korah rebelled against God and got other men to join him. What did God do to show His righteousness, 16.32,49? _____

2. He is righteous

_____

4. God is also holy; He hates sin and will not allow it to remain near Him. Only the priests could come near Him and only the Levites could serve in the Tabernacle. The laws for the priests and Levites teach that God is _____

3. He punished them and killed them.

_____

5. We also see in Numbers that God has great power. He provided food and water for the people and also performed a number of other miracles. For example, He made the ground open up and Korah and His followers all died, 16.32. How did God show His great power when He wanted to rebuke Balaam? _____

4. holy

_____

6. God caused Aaron's rod to grow flowers. What does this tell us about God? _____

5. He made the donkey speak like a man.

_____

7. God has all authority and can act according to His own will. In Numbers He chose the Levites, 3.41; Aaron, 16.5; and Moses, 12.6-8. God loves all His people but He has the _____ to choose those He wants to serve Him.

6. He has all power.

_____

8. God showed His love to Israel many times. He guided His people through the desert with a cloud. He also provided them with manna and water. These things prove that God has power and _____

7. authority

_____

4/6 9. God forgave His people Israel many times. What does this prove about the love of God? _____

8. love

_____

10. We have seen that Numbers teaches us that God is holy and righteous, loving and powerful; also that He has all authority. Write in the correct word about God after each of these six sentences.

9. It is very great.

  1. Ordinary men could not serve in the Tabernacle.   1. _____

  2. God told Israel to kill a man who gathered sticks on the Sabbath Day.   2. _____

  3. God can choose certain people to serve Him.   3. _____

  4. He made an ass speak to Balaam.   4. _____

72 Desert Journey

5. God often forgave His people. 5. _____

6. He also provided food and water for them in the desert. 6. _____

---

11. What about the Son of God? The name Christ is not found in the book of Numbers but there are pictures of Christ. For example, the Nazirite gave himself to serve God just because he wanted to do so. This makes us think of Christ who loved to do His Father's will. Moses was a very meek man, and this makes us think of Christ who also was _____

10. 1) Holiness
2) Righteousness
3) Authority
4) All power
5) Love
6) Love and power

---

12. Animals were killed for sacrifices: a picture of our Lord Jesus Christ when He _____

11. Gentle or meek, Matthew 11.29

---

13. The rock gave water when it was struck. It is a picture of Christ who died so that God can give _____ to all who believe.

12. died for us

---

14. Moses and Aaron prayed to God for the people of Israel. They were pictures of Christ as He _____ for His people today.

13. eternal life

---

15. Balaam was a false prophet but God made him say that a great leader like a star would rise up in Israel and give them victory over all their enemies, 24.17. God chose Joshua to lead His people to victory in the land of Canaan, 27.18. These things point forward to Christ when He will come back to win the _____ over all His enemies.

14. prays

---

16. All Scripture speaks of Christ and the book of Numbers also makes us think of Him in many different ways. Write in the correct words after each statement, 2 to 5.

15. victory

1. The Nazirite is a picture of Christ _____

2. The sacrifices are pictures of Christ. _____

3. The rock is a picture of Christ. _____

The Teaching of Numbers

4. Moses and Aaron are pictures of Christ. _____

5. Joshua is a picture of Christ. _____

4/7 17. Oil is a picture of the Holy Spirit because the Holy Spirit came on Christ, Matthew 3.16, just as oil was put on Aaron and the priests before they started their work for God, 4.16. Oil was also used with the sacrifices, 15.4, and through the Holy Spirit, Christ offered Himself as our Sacrifice, Hebrews 9.14. Oil often makes us think of God's _____

16. 1. He gave Himself to do His Father's will.
2. He died for us.
3. He gives the water of life.
4. He prays for His people.
5. He will gain the victory over all His enemies

18. In Numbers the Spirit came on Moses and the seventy elders, 11.17; and Joshua, 27.18. These were all men of God and today the Holy Spirit lives in the hearts of all believers. If you are a believer in Christ you can be sure that _____ lives in you.

17. Spirit

19. We also read that the Spirit came on Balaam, the false prophet, 24.2. The Spirit made Balaam say good things about Israel even when Balaam wanted to curse them so he could get a lot of money. We see that the Spirit has authority to come on any man and when He does, He can make him _____ according to God's will. (There are other spirits in the world and in Deuteronomy 32.17 we will read about false gods.)

18. the Holy Spirit

20. What does Numbers teach us about our salvation? We read that all parents had to redeem the first child in their family by paying five shekels of silver to the priest. In the New Testament we are set free by the blood of Christ, not by silver or gold, 1 Peter 1.18,19, but the five pieces of silver are a picture of the price of our _____

19. speak

21. After we are redeemed, we are sanctified. God bought us for Himself and now He wants us to be holy as He is holy, 1 Peter 1.15. So He sets us apart for Himself. We have pictures of this in Numbers. The Levites were set apart for God, 8.6,7. All Christians are like the Levites because God has _____ for Himself.

20. redemption

74 *Desert Journey*

22. God wants us to be clean and holy. The Israelite might become unclean but there was some water with ashes in it which would make him clean again, 19.9-12. Some people were unclean for a long time and they had to live outside the camp, 5.2. God wants us to learn these lessons and to live _____ lives.

21. set us apart

23. The book of Numbers teaches us many things about God and our Saviour; it also tells us a great deal about how we should live as Christians. We will think about three words which describe the life of the Christian: WALK, WAR, WORSHIP. The history of Israel teaches us how we should live as _____

22. clean and holy

Walk

24. God wanted Israel to walk and live according to His order. Each tribe knew where to set up their tents in the camp around the Tabernacle, chapter 2. This was the order of the _____

23. Christians

4/8 25. Each tribe knew which one should go first and which should follow next when they walked through the desert. This was the order of the _____ .

24. camp

26. From the New Testament we can learn God's _____ for our homes and churches.

25. journey

27. The people knew that they should get ready to leave when they heard the sound of the trumpet, 10.5-10. God showed them with a cloud where they should go and when they should stop. The trumpet told Israel _____ they should move, and the cloud showed them _____ they should go.

26. order

28. Today God guides us by His Word and by His Spirit. We can say that the _____ and the _____ are pictures of God's guidance.

27. when where

29. For a short time Israel followed the cloud and walked where God told them to go. They got to Kadesh-barnea but they refused to enter the land. Kadesh-barnea was a place of decision but the people made the _____ choice.

28. cloud trumpet

30. Then God made them go back and they walked in circles

29. wrong

The Teaching of Numbers 75

through the desert for 38 years. Israel refused to follow God at Kadesh-barnea and so they wasted many years before they could get back to the same place and enter the land God had promised them. A Christian may waste a lot of time because he makes the wrong _____.

---

31. Even after that 2½ tribes refused to enter the land and *30. decision* asked if they could live near it but not in it. Reuben, Gad and half of Manasseh are a picture of the Christian who is satisfied to have only _____ of God's blessing.

---

32. God still loved Israel even when they were walking in circles *31. part* in the desert. He provided them with manna and water and protected them with the cloud. We can see that God loves His people even when He has to _____ them for their sins.

War

¶/9 33. The people of Israel walked from Kadesh-barnea to the *32. punish* borders of the land which God had given them. They faced four nations on this part of their journey. First they asked the king of Edom to let them walk through his land but he refused and Israel had to walk a long way around it, 20.21. Edom would not _____ Israel.

---

34. Then they asked the king of the Amorites to let them walk *33. help* through his land. The Amorites also refused and then came out to fight against Israel, 21.23. Israel fought back, gained the victory, and took their land. The Amorites could not _____ Israel.

---

35. Then the king of Bashan tried to stop Israel but he also *34. defeat* was defeated, 21.33-35. The Midianites had already done Israel a great deal of harm so God told Israel to destroy them, 31.2. These four enemies treated Israel in different ways but they were all destroyed except _____.

---

36. Moses also had to struggle with some of the people inside the *35. one,* camp of Israel, but others stood with him. The people of Israel   *Edom* sinned or grumbled against God seven times in the book of Numbers.

1. They grumbled and the Lord sent _____ among them, 11.1-3.
2. They demanded that God should give them meat to eat and He did, but He also sent a terrible _____ among them, 11.4,31-33.
3. They disobeyed God at Kadesh-barnea and He made them _____

76 Desert Journey

around in the desert for 38 years, chapters 13 and 14.
4. Korah led many others to rebel against Moses and thousands of people _____, 16.33,49.
5. Another time they complained against God but God _____ Moses and Aaron because they were proud, 20.12.
6. They complained again and said they did not have either food or water. God sent _____ and many of the people died, 21.5,6.
7. The men of Israel worshipped the Baals and committed sin with the women of Moab until God sent another _____ among them, 25.1,9.

---

37. So we see that Moses had to face enemies from outside and enemies from _____ as well.

36. 1. Fire 2. disease 3. walk 4. died 5. punished 6. snakes 7. disease

---

38. Notice that the people of Israel were not fighting against Moses or among themselves when they saw the enemy nations from outside. We Christians today ought to be ready to fight against our enemies instead of fighting among _____.

37. inside

---

39. Israel had to fight against their enemies even when they were walking through the desert according to God's will. This shows that conflict is a normal part of the Christian life. But it is never God's will that we should be fighting with one another. Which kind of conflict is right, fighting with our outside enemies or with other believers? _____

38. ourselves

Worship

40. We should walk in the way God chooses and even if we must fight against our enemies He will surely give us victory over them. We also can worship God.

In Exodus we see that Israel built the Tabernacle, and in Leviticus God told them how to bring their sacrifices to the Tabernacle. Here in Numbers Israel walked through the desert and worshipped God at the Tabernacle. God arranged the Tabernacle and the sacrifices so the people of Israel could _____ Him according to His will.

39. with outside enemies

4/10 41. All Israelites could worship unless they were unclean but some of the Levites could come closer to the Tabernacle, 1.50.

40. worship

The Teaching of Numbers 77

There were 22,000 men and boys in the tribe of Levi; how many of them could serve in the Tabernacle? 4.46-48. _____

42. How many sons did Levi have? 3.17 _____ *41. 8,580*
How many grandsons did Levi have? 3.18-20. _____
What is the name of Levi's great grandson who had special privileges of worship as priest? 26.59 _____

43. Today all God's people are priests, 1 Peter 2.5, but many of *42. 3, 8* us do not really know how to worship God. We should thank God *Aaron* for saving us like the Samaritan leper who was cured by the Lord Jesus, Luke 17.12-19. All God's people today can worship Him as _____ but many fail to do so.

44. God wants us to praise Him. We should give thanks to God *43. priests* when He answers our prayers, Philippians 4.6. Moses asked God to take away the snakes so they would not bite more people and kill them. God answered his prayer and took away the snakes. God also showed Moses how the sick people could get better, 21.7-9. We see that God did _____ than Moses asked for.

45. In the same chapter the people praised the Lord with a *44. more* _____ when He gave them water, 21.17.

46. We can worship God by praising Him and by bringing Him our *45. song* gifts, Hebrews 13.15,16. God's law said that the people of Israel must bring a tenth of everything to Him. They could also bring gifts if they wanted to. For example the _____ brought their gifts to the Lord, 7.2. The _____ also brought an offering to the Lord, 31.48-50.

47. Can we learn any lessons from the history of Israel? *46. princes* All these things happened to Israel as _____ and as a *officers* _____ for us, 1 Corinthians 10.11.

47. examples
warning

Deuteronomy

		page
7	Moses' first message — Chapters 1-4	79
8	Moses' second message — Chapters 5-11	89

    The second law, Chapter 5
    Moses explained the first commandment, Chapter 6
    The Canaanites were destroyed, Chapter 7
    The journey through the desert, Chapter 8
    The things that happened to Israel in past years should be a warning to them, Chapters 9-11

9	Moses' second message cont. — Chapters 12-18	101

    Idol worship, Chapters 12, 13
    Israel must be separate from other nations, Chapter 14
    The seventh year, Chapter 15
    Three yearly feasts, 16.1-17
    Government, 16.18 - 17.20
    The portion of the Levites, 18.1-8
    Evil customs of the nations, 18.9-14
    The coming Prophet, 18.15-22

10	End of Moses' second message — Chapters 19-26	112

    Cities of safety, 19.1-14
    Witnesses, 19.15-21
    War, Chapter 20
    More instructions, Chapters 21, 22
    Holiness in the camp, 23.1-14
    Justice and mercy, Chapters 24, 25
    The end of Moses' second message, Chapter 26

11	Moses' third message — Chapters 27-30	124
	Moses' last words — Chapters 31-33	129

    Moses' last instructions to Israel, Chapter 31
    Moses' song, Chapter 32
    Moses blessed the tribes, Chapter 33
    Moses died and was buried, Chapter 34

12	The Teaching of Deuteronomy	138

MOSES' FIRST MESSAGE 7

The word **Deuteronomy** means "Second Law". This does not mean that God gave Israel another law to take the place of the one He had already given them in Exodus, Leviticus and Numbers. We find the Ten Commandments of Exodus 20 again in Deuteronomy 5.6-21, with small changes. Deuteronomy does not contain new laws and it does not just repeat the laws which God gave earlier. Instead the book of Deuteronomy explains these laws and commands Israel to obey them. The number 5 in the Bible often speaks of the fact that man must give an account of his life to God. The fifth book of the Bible teaches this truth very plainly.

Few people learn a lesson well the first time and every good teacher knows that he must go over the lesson again and again. The Law of God is very important. Because of this God wanted to repeat it, explain it, and add more detail to it. This is what we have in the book of Deuteronomy.

But the Holy Spirit does not just say the same thing again. For example, the books of Chronicles tell again part of the history of Judah which had been written in the books of Samuel and Kings, but in Chronicles we see especially the spiritual side of these events. The Gospel of John tells the story of the Lord Jesus Christ which had already been written by Matthew, Mark, and Luke, but John shows us especially that the Lord Jesus Christ is God. He gives us many additional details which help us to understand the other three Gospels better. Deuteronomy also tells us more details about what we have read before and points out the spiritual side and tells how these things should apply to the life of the reader.

Moses wrote most of Deuteronomy. The Lord Jesus used verses from Deuteronomy when He spoke to the people. Read the following verses together:

Matthew 4.4	and	Deuteronomy 8.3
Matthew 4.7	and	Deuteronomy 6.16
Matthew 4.10	and	Deuteronomy 6.13
Matthew 22.37	and	Deuteronomy 6.5

In this way Christ showed that God led and inspired Moses to write this book. Paul also used verses from Deuteronomy in his letters: Romans 12.19 is from 32.35; Galatians 3.10 is from 27.26.

    Who taught that Moses wrote Deuteronomy 18.15? Acts 7.37 (Write in your answer) _____

    Who taught that Moses wrote Deuteronomy 24.1? Matthew 19.8 _____

    Who taught that Moses wrote Deuteronomy 32.21? Romans 10.19 _____

Some people say that Moses did not write Deuteronomy. They teach that someone else wrote it hundreds of years later. They say that Christ did not know any more than the other Jews who lived at that time. Some say that Christ spoke as if Moses wrote Deuteronomy because His disciples thought so and He did not want to argue with them. Those who love the Lord Jesus Christ believe that He is the Son of God (as Peter did, Matthew 16.16; John 6.68). They also accept the words of the Lord Jesus rather than the teachings of men. We can be sure that Moses wrote the book of Deuteronomy. We are also sure that God inspired him to write what he did and that God is speaking to us in this book. May we read, learn and obey His commands!

Most of Deuteronomy consists of three messages which Moses gave to the people of Israel when they were on the east side of the River Jordan. Two of these messages were short and one was long.

    1.   In the first message Moses reminded the people of the things that had happened to them since they first became a nation, chapters 1-4.

    2.   In the second message he told them to keep the Law, chapters 5-26.

    3.   In the third message he told them God would send them either curses or blessings, chapters 27,28.

    4.   In chapters 29 and 30 he renewed their covenant with the Lord.

5. In chapters 31 to 33 we read Moses' last words, his song, and his blessing on the different tribes of Israel.
6. Chapter 34 tells about Moses' death and burial.

All these things happened in about five weeks or less. Moses began to speak to Israel on the first day of the eleventh month of the fortieth year after they were delivered from Egypt, 1.3. After Moses died the people grieved for him for 30 days, 34.8. On the tenth day of the first month they crossed the Jordan river and entered the land of Canaan, Joshua 4.19. So Moses died no later than the eighth day of the twelfth month. So in Deuteronomy we read what Moses said in the four weeks of the eleventh month and the first week of the twelfth month.

	Day	Month	Read
1. Israel crossed the river Jordan	10	1	Joshua 4.19
2. Israel mourned for Moses for thirty days after he died, so he must have died before	10	12	Deut. 34.8
3. Moses started to speak to Israel about five weeks before he died	1	11	Deut. 1.3

MOSES' FIRST MESSAGE, chapters 1-4

4/11 The first five verses of chapter 1 tell **where** Moses and the Israelites were when he give them the messages contained in this book. Verse 3 also informs us **when** he began to speak to them. First of all Moses reminded the Israelites of the things that happened to them as they journeyed from Mount Horeb to the land of Bashan, 1.6 - 3.29, and then appealed to them to obey the commands of God.

Where were the Israelites at the beginning of Deuteronomy? 1.1-5

At this time the people had put up their tents in the valley of Beth-peor, 3.29; 4.46. Horeb is another name for Mount Sinai where God gave Moses the Law, 5.2. People could make the journey from Mount Horeb to Kadesh-barnea in only eleven days, **1.2.** Why did the Holy Spirit lead Moses to mention this here?

God had commanded Israel to leave Mount Sinai on the twentieth day of the second month of the second year, Numbers 10.11. The people could have been on the borders of the land 11 days later, early in the third month. They did get to Kadesh-barnea, but they did not believe that God could give them the land of Canaan, so they turned back and wandered around in the desert for 38 years. Instead of 11 days they had to wait 38 years.

Many believers have wasted precious years of their lives because they did not believe God and therefore made a wrong decision. There are many practical lessons for us in the book of Deuteronomy, like this one in verse 2. Moses taught the people of Israel these things and the Holy Spirit wants us to learn them too.

Moses began to speak to Israel on the first day of the eleventh month, **1.3**. The people offered special offerings at the beginning of each month, Numbers 28.11. Moses had led the people when they defeated Sihon and Og, **v.4**, and they should have been glad to listen to him. He began to explain the Law to them in verse **5**, but most of this explanation is in Moses' second message, chapters 5 to 26. First of all Moses reminded the people of what had happened to them during the past years.

Horeb, 1.6-18

4/12 Moses reminded Israel that the Lord had commanded them to leave Horeb and go to the mountain country of the Amorites, that is, Kadesh-barnea, 1.7,19. Then he said that he himself was not at all able to settle all the quarrels and arguments of the people, vs.9, 12.

Those who try to help and teach the people of God must remember that they themselves are weak, Galatians 6.1.

At two different times people were chosen to help Moses govern the nation, Exodus 18.24-26; Numbers 11.16. The first group were chosen after Moses' father-in-law suggested that Moses needed help. This was before God gave the Law at Mount Sinai. God told Moses to choose the second group when Moses complained about having too much work after they left Sinai and before they came to Kadesh-barnea.

In verses 9 to 18 Moses was thinking of both these occasions. In Numbers 11 the Holy Spirit came only on 70 elders of Israel. There were over 600,000 men in Israel, so there were 60,000 commanders of units of ten people, Exodus 18.25; Deuteronomy 1.15, and many other officers as well. In verse 15 Moses was thinking about the first group of officers. He had commanded these officers and judges to judge righteously, vs.16,17.

Kadesh-barnea, 1.19-46

4/13 Moses had commanded them to enter the land when they got to Kadesh-barnea, and he promised that God would help them. We now learn that it was the people who first wanted to send men into the land of Canaan to find out what the country was like. Moses agreed, 1.23, and the first two verses in Numbers 13 seem to show that he asked the Lord about it. The Lord told him to send the men, but this should not have been necessary. God had already told the people that the land was good. It did not matter whether the people of the land were strong or not because God would have helped the Israelites to drive them out anyway. So the spies were sent because the people did not believe God.

They brought back a bad report and the people refused to obey the Lord and enter the land, **1.26**. Moses, Joshua and Caleb tried to persuade the people to obey, but they refused. The Lord swore that all the adults then living would die except Caleb and Joshua, who would go into the land, **vs.36,38**. God would also allow the children to enter and the young people who were less than 20 years old at this time, **v.39**; Numbers 14.29.

God commanded the people to go back into the desert by the way of the Red Sea, **1.40**. They obeyed, 2.1, and so came back to the Red Sea the third time. God had wonderfully delivered them the first time they were there, Exodus 13.18. He brought them back the second time, Numbers 33.10, and the third time to remind them of His power and that it was a dangerous thing for them to disobey Him.

4/14 While at Kadesh-barnea the Israelites tried to fight against the Amorites without the Lord's help, but the Amorites drove them away as bees, **1.41-44**. Then the people were very sorry for what they had done and wept before the Lord, v.45, but God did not take away their punishment.

> Sometimes God does not punish Christians when they repent, but if they make their hearts hard, they must accept His punishment and understand that it comes from their loving heavenly Father. David is an example of this, 2 Samuel 12.13,14.

So in Deuteronomy 1 we see that the people disobeyed God, v.26; they grumbled, v.27; they refused to believe God, v.32, and acted as if they did not need God's help, v.43. These things should be a warning to us.

Seir, 2.1-7

4/15 So Israel wandered in the desert for 38 years. Then they came near the land of the descendants of Esau, and God told them not to take their country. God had given this land to the descendants of Esau and Israel should pay for any food and water they might get from them. Esau is also called Edom, Genesis 36.1. In Numbers 20.14-21 we see that the Israelites tried to pay the Edomites for food and water, but the Edomites did not allow them to pass through their land.

Moab, 2.8-15

God had also given land to the descendants of Moab who was one of the sons of Lot, Genesis 19.36,37. These people were able to overcome giants and take this land, and Israel did the same to Og and Bashan, v.12. However the adults of the nation of Israel all died in the desert because they had refused to obey God, 2.14. Some of them were less than 60 years old when they died. Only Moses, Caleb and Joshua were over 58 years old at this time. At the end of the 38 years the rest of the people were ready to enter and take the land of Canaan.

Ammon, 2.16-23

4/16 God also told the Israelites not to trouble the Ammonites, who were the descendants of Ben-ammi, Lot's other son, Genesis 19.38. God had helped them to defeat the giants in the land which He had given them. The Lord wanted this to encourage the people of Israel. These giants had different names, but to us they are a picture of everything that tries to keep us from following the Lord.

Heshbon, 2.24-37

4/17 God had told Israel not to trouble the Edomites, Moabites and Ammonites. Now they came to the land which God had given them. God said He would begin to make other nations afraid when they heard about the Israelites, v.25. Why then did Moses send a friendly message to Sihon and ask him to allow them to pass through their land and buy food and water? Moses' words suggest that the Edomites had allowed them to go through their land, v.29, but this was not true, Numbers 20.18,20,21. The Lord hardened Sihon's heart, v.30, and enabled the Israelites to defeat him and his people, vs.32,33. But even so Moses had done wrong because he had acted in a friendly way toward Sihon.

Our enemies are our bad habits which lead us into sin. We should learn to hate sin and fight against anything which leads us into sin.

Bashan, 3.1-20

4/18 Then the Lord commanded Israel to take the land of Bashan. Og, the king, tried to fight against them, but he was killed together with his people, Numbers 21.33-35. The people of Israel destroyed sixty cities which had walls around them and many villages. They killed all the people, but left their cattle alive. Og was also a giant: he had an iron bed which was 13½ feet long, v.11.

4/19 The lands of Heshbon and Bashan are also called Mount Gilead or the hill country of Gilead. Moses gave the land of Heshbon to the Reubenites and the Gadites, and Bashan to the half tribe of Manasseh, but he reminded them that they must cross the Jordan river with the other tribes and help them take the land of Canaan, 3.18-20.

Moses encouraged Joshua, 3.21-29

4/20 Moses reminded Joshua that the Lord had helped them before to defeat their enemies and told him not to be afraid of other enemies whom they would have to fight later on. Moses asked God to allow him to enter the land, 3.25, and was very sad because the Lord refused, 1.37; 4.21. Moses was a great man of faith, but here he prayed for a certain thing and God did not give him what he asked for.

Paul also asked the Lord three times to take away from him a physical weakness that caused him pain, but the Lord did not do it. Why? Because His power was strongest when Paul was weak, 2 Corinthians 12.8,9. God cannot use anyone who is proud, and this physical weakness kept Paul from becoming proud.

God did not do what Moses asked for because He is righteous and had to punish Moses for disobeying Him, Numbers 20.7-12. So God told Moses he could look at the land from the top of Mount Pisgah, v.27. A few weeks later Moses did this just before he died, 34.1-4. Here God commanded him again to encourage Joshua to lead the people into Canaan, 3.28.

Why should we be sad if God does not give us what we ask Him for? We know that He loves us and that He works all things out for our good, Romans 8.28. We should therefore thank God even when He answers our prayer with "No". God always answers our prayers, but sometimes it seems to us as if He did not answer, but this is because we do not understand His perfect ways.

Moses told the people not to worship idols, 4.1-40

4/21 Moses had been reminding Israel how righteously God had acted toward them in past years and that He had done wonderful things for them. Now he told them that these things should cause them to obey the Lord. Moses did not think he was a good speaker when God first called him, Exodus 4.10, but here in Deuteronomy we see that he had become a very great speaker, one of the best who have ever lived. God had taught him many things and had given him this gift and Moses used it to teach the people and draw them closer to the Lord.

First he told them to obey all the commands of God without adding any other laws to them, **4.1,2**. Then he reminded them how God had judged them at Baal-peor, Numbers 25.5. Israel was different from the other nations because God was among them and had given them His laws, **vs.6-9**. God showed that He was among them when Mount Horeb burned with fire, **v.11**, and the Lord gave Moses the Ten Commandments, **v.14**. Because of these things Israel was separate from all other nations.

4/22 Moses also warned the people against worshipping idols or images of any kind, **4.15-24**. They had not seen God on Mount Horeb so they could not make an image to represent Him. God told them not to make an image of man or woman, or any animal or bird or fish, vs.16-18. He also commanded them not to worship the sun, moon or stars which the Lord had given to all men to show them what time of day and of year it is, Genesis 1.14. Moses told them again about what had happened to himself to show them that God is righteous, vs.21,22. They must not worship any image because God is a jealous God and is like a great fire which burns up everything, vs.23,24.

4/23 In verses **25** to **31** Moses warned the people that God would judge them if they disobeyed. If they began to worship idols, some of them would die, v.26, and the rest would have to go and live among the people of other nations, v.27. Even then God would not leave them if they were sorry for their sins and came back to Him, vs.29-31.

The people of Israel should remember that God had dealt with them more wonderfully than with any other nation. God had never spoken to any other nation out of a mountain burning with fire, **4.33,36**, and He had never delivered any people from another nation as He had delivered Israel out of Egypt, **v.34**. He had driven out great nations to make a place for His own people, **v.38**. God had given land to Esau, Moab and Ammon, 2.5,9,19, but He gave a much better land to Israel. So Moses commanded Israel to obey Jehovah and no one else. If they did so, they would get on well in the land and live long lives, **vs.39,40**.

We too should obey God because He is God. He has spoken to us through the most wonderful book which has ever been written, the Holy Bible. We too were slaves, not of the Egyptians but of sin, and God delivered us. He did not bring us into the land of Canaan, but into a place of much greater blessing. We have been justified by the blood of Christ, set apart for God by the Holy Spirit, and blessed with all spiritual blessings, Romans 5.9; 15.10; Ephesians 1.3.

Cities to run to for safety, 4.41-43

4/24 When Moses had finished his first message, he named three cities on the east side of the Jordan river to which a person could run and be safe if he had accidentally killed another person. By naming these three cities Moses partly fulfilled the Lord's command in Numbers 35.9-15. Later three more cities were chosen, Joshua 20.7.

The last verses of the chapter, verses **44 to 49**, prepare us for Moses' second and longest message, chapters 5 to 26. He gave Israel this message in the valley of Beth-peor, 4.46, after Israel had defeated the two kings, Og and Sihon. In this message he taught the people about the laws and commands and judgments of God, vs.44,45.

TEST YOURSELF - Deuteronomy chapters 1-4
1. Why does the Spirit tell us it was only eleven days journey from Sinai to Kadesh-barnea?
2. How many men did God give Moses to help him govern the people?
3. How old were the oldest people who entered Canaan, except Caleb and Joshua?
4. Which countries were protected from Israel?
5. Which nations were not protected?
6. Why did God refuse to answer Moses' prayer?
7. How did Moses become a good speaker?
8. What kind of images could Israel worship, men, women, animals, fish or birds, or God Himself?
9. How did God show that He loved Israel?
10. How does God show that He loves us?
11. Moses named only three cities of refuge, all east of the Jordan river. What was provided in the land of Canaan for any man who killed someone by accident? *Turn to page 148 to check your answers.*

MOSES' SECOND MESSAGE

8

4/25 In the book of Deuteronomy we see Moses using the gift which God had given him, the gift for speaking in public to many people. This message is full of commands and appeals and it is difficult to divide it in an orderly way. Perhaps Moses gave it all on one day or at different times during several days, but the message goes right on to the end of chapter 26 without a break or stopping point.

The second law, chapter 5

At the beginning of his second message Moses repeated the Ten Commandments which had already been given in Exodus 20. He reminded the people that years ago God had spoken to them from the mountain and had made an agreement with them. At that time many of them were still children and young people, 5.5.

The Ten Commandments here in Deuteronomy 5 are almost the same as those in Exodus 20. The only important difference is the reason given for the Fourth Commandment. In Exodus 20.11 God told the people to rest on the sabbath because Jehovah had made heaven and earth in six days and rested on the seventh day. In Deuteronomy 5.15 He told them to keep the sabbath because He had delivered them with great power from being slaves in Egypt. Jehovah destroyed the first born children in Egypt on the fourteenth day of the first month which was a sabbath day, Exodus 12.28,29. So in Exodus God told them to keep the sabbath to remind them that He had created the world, and in Deuteronomy, that He had redeemed them from being slaves.

4/26 There are other small additions in Deuteronomy:

Exodus 20	Deuteronomy 5
In verse 8 they were told to **remember** the sabbath day.	In verse 12 they were told to **keep** the sabbath day as the Lord had commanded them to do, and in verse 14 we read that the animals should not work and the servants would be able to rest as well as their masters.
Verse 12 commanded them to honour their parents.	Verse 16 told them a reason for doing so - that it might go well with them.

God had spoken these commands to all the people and written them on two flat pieces of stone, **5.22**.

The people were very much afraid when they saw God's power at Mount Sinai. God had spoken to them and they had not died, but they asked that they might not hear His voice again, **5.25**. They wanted Moses to go and listen to God's words, and promised to do whatever God commanded them, **v.27**. They did not really understand what God was like and thought He might suddenly turn against them and destroy them. They also did not understand that they were not able to keep the law of God.

4/27 Jehovah was willing for Moses to stand between Him and the people, but He knew that the people would not be able to keep their promise to obey Him, **5.29**. In the last two verses He strongly commanded them again to obey Him and promised that they would live long lives if they did so. He did this also in the last two verses of Moses' first message, **4.39,40**.

Moses explained the first commandment, chapter 6

4/28 The first commandment told the people not to worship any other gods, **5.7**. Chapter 6 gives more details about this. God gave His people all these commands and laws so that they might obey them, fear Him, live long and be successful, **6.1-3**.

Even today the Jews use verses 4 and 5 to teach that there is only one God. Christians also believe that there is only one God, but the New Testament teaches also that He is

Father, Son and Holy Spirit. Words like "Hear, O Israel," v.4, are found again and again in this book; see 4.1; 5.1; 6.4; 9.1; 20.3; 27.9.

The Lord Jesus called verse 5 the greatest and most important command, Matthew 22.37,38, and the way to get life, Luke 10.27,28. Jehovah did everything He could to make the people of Israel love Him, Isaiah 43.1-4. He has done even more for us because He has revealed Himself more fully to us. A person who has not been born again cannot love God because he does not know Him. The Law could command men to do certain things, but it could not give them the power to do them. God gave men the Law to prove to them that they are not at all able to please Him.

When people learn this they begin to understand how much they need God's mercy and grace. See Romans 7.7-25; Galatians 3.19-25. The Holy Spirit causes us to love God, Romans 5.5; Galatians 5.22; 1 Peter 1.8. The Lord Jesus Christ had prayed that it might be so, John 17.26. We will love God more and more as we spend time with Him in prayer, and as we think about His Word and the work which Christ has done for us.

Here in Deuteronomy God commanded the people to remember His words, **6.6**, to teach them to their children, and to talk about them throughout the day. Even today some Jews really try to obey the law and they tie a little portion of Scripture in a place where it can be easily seen, **vs.8,9**. Of course this cannot take the place of really knowing God through the Lord Jesus Christ.

Then Moses warned the people not to forget the Lord when they were living in the land of Canaan and had everything they needed, **6.10-15**.

4/29 When Satan tempted the Lord Jesus, the Lord used three verses from the Bible to defeat him. These verses are found in Deuteronomy 6.13,16 and 8.3. This fact shows us how important the Word of God and the book of Deuteronomy are. In Matthew 4.10 and Luke 4.8 Jesus said that we must worship and serve only the Lord our God. These words are almost the same as those in

Deuteronomy 6.13. Perhaps the Lord Jesus was also thinking of 1 Samuel 7.3. Christ used these words when Satan told Him to fall down and worship him. Satan was only a creature and God has commanded men not to worship any creature or idol, so Jesus as a man commanded Satan to go away, Matthew 4.10.

God did not want the Israelites to fear any other gods or swear by their names. To swear here means to call on God to judge him if he is not telling the truth or if he does not do what he promised to do. The Lord Jesus Christ and the Holy Spirit through the apostle James both commanded us not to swear, Matthew 5.34-37; James 5.12.

The Lord also used verse 16 to defeat Satan. Satan tempted the Lord Jesus by telling Him to throw Himself down from the top of the temple. The people would think this was a wonderful thing to do. Satan used verses 11 and 12 of Psalm 91 to prove to the Lord Jesus that God would tell His angels to care for the Messiah. It is true that this promise in Psalm 91 is for the Messiah if He should have an accident, but it is quite wrong for someone to put God to the test to see if He will fulfil His promise. The people of Israel put God to the test like this when they asked Him to give them some meat, Psalm 78.18-20.

How do these things apply to us? God has promised to keep us from committing sin, but we must not of our own free will go to places where we will be tempted to sin. The Lord Jesus taught us to pray, *Lead us not into temptation,* Matthew 6.13.

A son might come to his father to ask about the rules and laws. The father would explain that Jehovah had delivered them from Egypt, **6.21,22**, had brought them to the land which He had promised to give them, **v.23**, and had commanded them to obey these laws. This would be good for them and help them to live righteous lives, **vs.24,25**. It is very important for parents to teach their children about the Lord so that they will learn to love and obey Him, Ephesians 6.4. There are also Sunday Schools in many places where Christian teachers teach the Word of God to children who do not have a Christian father and mother. It is very important not to turn a child away from the Lord, **Matthew** 18.6.

The Canaanites were destroyed, chapter 7

4/30 The name Canaan is used for the whole land which God promised to give to Israel, but at that time six other nations lived in it besides the Canaanites. The Lord God said that He would help Israel to defeat these nations and commanded Israel not to show them any mercy. He told them not to marry anyone belonging to these seven nations because these people would draw them away from the Lord. God also commanded the Israelites to destroy all their idols and everything that had to do with their worship of idols, **7.5**.

Jehovah had chosen Israel to be a holy people, **7.6-11**. He did not choose them because they were a larger nation as they were only 70 people when they went down to Egypt, **10.22**. The Lord chose Israel because He loved them and because of the promise He had made to their ancestors, **v.8**. God is righteous and keeps His agreement with those who love Him, **v.9**, and He punishes those who hate Him, **v.10**.

5/1 Then Moses told them more about the blessing they would receive if they obeyed God, **7.12-16**. The Lord would keep His agreement and would love and bless them more than all other people. They would have many children and good farms, v.13. They would be healthy, v.15, and defeat their enemies, v.16. God does not promise Christians any of these things now, but He has blessed us greatly. The obedient child of God may not have a large family, but he may have the joy of leading others to Christ. (Paul and John called Christians their children, Galatians 4.19; 1 John 2.1.) The Christian may not have much money but he will get on well spiritually and be filled with the joy of the Lord. It is better for a person to be strong spiritually than physically and that person will certainly be able to overcome the temptations of Satan in his life.

Then Moses told Israel that God would give them the victory, **7.17-26**. They should remember what God had done in Egypt, vs.18,19, and that He is able to do anything He wants to do. He could destroy the nations in the land of Canaan in a moment, but He chose to put them out slowly, v.22, so that Israel could occupy the land and keep the wild animals from becoming too many. They would take the land gradually, but would have complete victory in the end. Moses also commanded them very strongly to destroy all the idols in the land. If they did not do this, these idols would become a curse to them, vs.25,26.

A Christian may not be able to overcome every sinful habit in his life the day he accepts the Lord Jesus Christ, just as the nations of Canaan were not destroyed in one day. The new Christian might not even understand at first that some of his habits are sinful, but as he gets to know the Lord more and more, the Lord will enable him to overcome these things.

Many Christians do not enjoy all the blessings of the Lord because they continue to do something which they know is a sin. Perhaps they become angry quickly, or are not quite honest in what they say or do, or do not really trust God. God will reveal to us any sin in our lives if we ask Him to do so, and He will help us to overcome it.

The journey through the desert, and the promised land, chapter 8

5/2 Moses told the people why God had led them through the desert. The Lord wanted to humble them and to test them to see if they would really obey Him, 8.2. He allowed them to be hungry and then fed them with manna so that they might learn a great truth. This truth is that man cannot live only on bread, but also needs every word that God speaks, **v.3**.

The Lord Jesus used these words to answer Satan when Satan tempted Him the first time, Matthew 4.4; Luke 4.4. Millions of people spend all their time getting things for their bodies, such as food and clothes and other things. These things help our bodies, but we can get true life, eternal life, only through the Word of God, 1 Peter 1.23.

As the people of Israel journeyed through the desert, their clothes did not wear out and their feet did not become too tired to walk, **8.4**. They had many difficult experiences because God was teaching them and punishing them. This proved that He loved them, Hebrews 12.6.

Moses also reminded them of the blessings which God had promised to give them in the future. He described all the good things they would find in the land, **8.7-10**: plenty of water, grain and fruit, oil and honey, also different kinds of metal in the rocks of the hills, v.9. They must remember to thank the Lord for these things, v.10.

5/3 They should also be careful not to forget the Lord their God, **8.11-20**. He would give the people more than what they needed, vs.11-13. Then it would be very easy for them to forget how the Lord had delivered them, vs.14-16, and to think that they had obtained all these things by their own efforts, vs.17,18. Some of them would forget God and start to worship idols. God would destroy them just as the nations whom the Lord was going to put out of the land before Israel, vs.19,20.

In the New Testament the apostle Paul warned us not to love money because it is a source of all kinds of evil. Those who are rich should trust God and help others, 1 Timothy 6.10, 17-19.

It is easy for us to forget God even when He has been giving us special blessing. It seems that we often want to take a little glory to ourselves. This is why many Christians fail and are defeated after the Lord has blessed their service for Him. We should remember that Satan makes a special effort to destroy the work of God just at a time like that.

The things that happened to Israel in past years should be a warning to them, chapters 9-11

5/4 The messengers had told Israel that the promised land was a good land but that they would not be able to take it. The people of the land were greater, taller and stronger than the Israelites and their cities had high walls around them, 1.28; **9.1,2**. The Lord was going to give Israel the victory and Moses warned them in advance that they must not take glory to themselves for this. God would give Israel the land because the nations were very wicked, not because the people of Israel were righteous, **v.4**; in fact they were very stubborn, **v.6**. God also wanted to fulfil His promise to their ancestors, **v.5**.

In the rest of the chapter we see why Moses called Israel a stubborn people. He reminded them what had happened at Horeb and Kadesh. Moses had climbed Mount Horeb and there he did not eat any food for 40 days. At the end God gave him the two flat stones on which He had written the Law, **9.9**. The first and second commandments of the Law told the people not to worship any god or idol or any creature. They must worship only Jehovah. The people had promised before that they would obey the laws, 5.27, but they broke them even before Moses got down from the mountain. The Lord told Moses that they had already made an idol, **v.12**.

5/5 God wanted to test Moses so He told him that He would destroy Israel and start a greater nation with Moses' children, **9.13,14**. Moses came down from the mountain and saw the calf made of gold, **9.16**. He broke the two stones on which the Law had been written because the people of Israel had already broken the Law. Then he spent another 40 days and nights without eating while he prayed for Israel and asked God not to destroy them, Exodus 32.11-13. Aaron was also guilty, but God did not destroy him because Moses prayed for him.

We too have a Great High Priest who is always praying for us, Hebrews 7.25. Let us praise God for the Lord Jesus Christ, our Saviour.

Moses took the calf, burned it in the fire, pounded the gold and ground it into powder. He put some of this powder into water and made the people drink it, Exodus 32.20. The rest of the powder he threw into the brook, Deuteronomy 9.21.

This was not the only time the people had rebelled against God. They disobeyed the Lord also at Taberah, Numbers 11.1,3, at Massah, Exodus 17.7, at Kibroth-hattaavah, Numbers 11.34, and especially at Kadesh-barnea, **9.22,23**. They had been rebels right from the beginning, **9.24**. Stephen said that they continued to rebel against God right up to the time when the Lord Jesus Christ came to earth, Acts 7.51-53. The Church also has not obeyed the Lord. Of course there are always some people who really want to obey God and do His will, but there are many more who disobey.

Moses' prayer for the people reminded the Lord that He had redeemed Israel, His own people, out of Egypt, **9.26**. If He did not bring them into the land of Canaan, the Egyptians would say that

He did not love Israel and did not have the power to bring them into the land, v.28. The Lord called Israel the *people of Moses* whom Moses had brought out of Egypt, v.12, but Moses called them *the people of God* whom the Lord had brought out of Egypt, v.29!

5/6   The Lord agreed to do what Moses had asked and told him to bring two more flat stones on which He would write the same commandments again. He had already told Moses how to build the Tabernacle and make its furniture. One of these pieces of furniture was the ark, a box of acacia wood, Exodus 25.10,11, which was covered with gold. Here in Deuteronomy we learn that Moses made an ark of wood at this time just to carry the two flat stones of the Law until the real ark was prepared, 10.1-5.

The wooden ark covered with gold is a picture of Christ. Wood is a common thing and reminds us that He humbled Himself, Philippians 2.8; Matthew 11.29. Gold is very precious and so it teaches that Christ is God. The Law was placed inside the ark. This reminds us that the Lord Jesus Christ kept the law of God in His heart, and never departed from it, Psalm 37.31.

In verses 6 and 7 of chapter 10 we read of the journeys of Israel to several places, and about the death of Aaron. In Numbers 33.38 we learn that Aaron climbed Mount Hor and died there. It seems that the hill country around the mountain was also called Hor. This is where Beeroth, Moserah, Gudgodah and Jotbathah were located. We also learn from Numbers 33.32,34 that Israel had been to several of these places. Perhaps they made another journey and then came back again to these four places mentioned in Deuteronomy 10.6,7.

Moses had been telling the people how they had rebelled against God and how he had prayed for them at Mount Sinai. Why did he tell about Aaron's death before continuing with this story in verses **8-11**?

Aaron died 38 years after God chose the tribe of Levi, 10.8. Moses mentioned it here to remind his hearers of several things:
1. They were not able to keep the Law and needed a priest.
2. God would judge the priest also if he did not obey Him.

3. Some of the Levites had failed, but even so men from the tribe of Levi would continue to be priests.
4. God arranged for Eleazar to become high priest after his father's death.
5. Aaron died at Mosera, v.6. From there Israel journeyed on to the land of many rivers of waters, v.7. This was a picture of how they could go on to be blessed even more.

Today Christians are not under the law, but they still need a High Priest and have a much greater One than Aaron. Our Lord Jesus Christ will never die again and does not need anyone to take His place, but leads His people into far greater blessing than the people of Israel ever enjoyed.

At Mount Sinai Moses destroyed the golden calf, but some of the people who had worshipped it still did not put on their clothes again. This was part of the evil practice of the other nations and showed that they were not at all sorry for what they had done. Moses asked those who loved the Lord to destroy these people, and the men of the tribe of Levi did so, Exodus 32.25-29. They set themselves apart for God and God blessed them with special privileges. This is what Moses referred to at the beginning of verse 8, but we can read more about it in Numbers. Then Moses climbed the mountain again and stayed there for 40 days and 40 nights without food or water, v.10; Exodus 34.28.

5/7 Because of these things Moses asked the question, *What does the Lord your God ask of you?* **10.12.** The Lord wanted them to fear Him, to walk in His ways, to love Him, serve Him, and keep His commandments, vs.12,13. The prophet Micah asked this question also and answered it in Micah 6.8. God created this whole world and it belongs to Him, but He chose Abraham, Isaac and Jacob. Therefore Israel must "circumcise the heart," **v.16.** This means that they should treat their own sinful nature as if it were dead and leave their sins and love the Lord.

Jehovah is God of gods and Lord of lords, **10.17.** He will protect children who do not have any parents and give them what they need. He will do the same for widows and strangers. The Israelites should love and help strangers because they themselves

Deuteronomy 10, 11   99

had been strangers in Egypt. Now there were very many people in Israel, as many as the stars. God had promised Abraham that it would be so, Genesis 15.5.

5/8   God is great and men should love and obey Him. He will punish those who disobey and Moses was speaking to Israelites who had seen how God punishes His people. When they were still children, they had seen the miracles in Egypt and at the Red Sea, **11.3,4**. They had been there when God punished Dathan and Abiram, **vs.5-7**. Numbers 16.1,31. If Israel obeyed, they would be strong, possess the land and live long, **vs.8,9**.

This land was not like Egypt where there is no rain and where water must be brought from the river Nile to make the grain grow. God took care of the land of Canaan during the whole year, **11.10-12**. If the people obeyed the Lord, they would have rain in the proper seasons, good crops, and plenty of food, **vs.13-15**. However if they served idols, God would not allow the rain to fall, **vs.16,17**. They should always remember Moses' words and teach them to their children and write them on the door posts of their houses, **vs.18-20**. Moses had already said these things in 4.9 and 6.6. Now he added that God would give them success and they would live long lives, **v.21**.

5/9   The Lord also promised to give the Israelites the victory over the nations of Canaan if they obeyed Him, **11.22-25**; 4.38; 9.1-3.

The New Testament does not promise that Christians will succeed in this world, but it does tell us that heaven for the Christian is to be with Christ which is far better than anything here on earth, Philippians 1.23; Revelation 21.22 - 22.5.

God deals with men in different ways in different ages and makes agreements with them which are also called *covenants*. God made two kinds of covenants with men, conditional and unconditional. In the *unconditional* covenant God promised to do something, but men did not have to do anything. For instance, God promised Abraham that He would cause his descendants to become a great nation, Genesis 12.2,3. This was an unconditional promise or covenant. We live in the period of God's grace, and He has promised to save anyone who believes in Christ. A person does not have to do any good works in order to be saved. Here we have another example of an unconditional covenant.

The covenant of the Law however was *conditional.* God promised to do certain things IF Israel would obey. We can see this very clearly in the last part of chapter 11. Moses put before Israel a blessing and a curse. God would bless them if they obeyed His commandments and He would curse them if they did not obey, **11.26-28.** Moses told them to set aside Mount Gerizim for the blessing and Mount Ebal for the curse when they came into the land, **vs.29-32.** We will read more about this command in 27.11 to 28.68; and in Joshua 8.33,34 we see that Joshua obeyed it.

TEST YOURSELF - Deuteronomy chapters 5 - 11

1. In Exodus 20, what was the reason for keeping the sabbath? What was it in Deuteronomy 5?
2. Did Israel understand God or themselves at Sinai?
3. Which is the greatest commandment? Who said so?
4. What kind of people can love the Lord God?
5. What verses did the Lord Jesus use to defeat Satan?
6. Why did God choose Israel for special blessings?
7. How did God promise to bless Christians?
8. Why did God allow His people to remain hungry?
9. What should we do when the Lord gives us a time of special blessing?
10. Why did God say He would drive the Canaanites out of the land?
11. Why did Moses call Israel stubborn?
12. How does the Ark make us think of Christ?
13. What does it mean to circumcise the heart?
14. Give an example of a conditional covenant and of an unconditional covenant.

Turn to page 148 to check your answers.

MOSES' SECOND MESSAGE cont'd   9

In the first part of his second message, chapters 5-11, Moses urged the people very strongly to obey God's commands. In the second part of his message, chapters 12-26, he explained some of these commands more fully.

Idol worship, chapters 12,13

5/10   We can think of these two chapters as an explanation of the second commandment. When the people of Israel came into the land, God wanted them to destroy all the places where the people of the land had offered sacrifices to their idols. He commanded Israel to break their altars, destroy the idols and burn the trees which grew around these places, **12.2,3**.

The Israelites were not allowed to offer sacrifices to God at any of these places. God wanted them to bring their offerings to a central place. He Himself would choose the place where He wanted them to worship Him. This was very important and Moses referred to it at least eighteen times in chapters 12 to 18. However he did not say where this place would be. While Joshua led the people of Israel, the Tabernacle was set up at **Shiloh**, Joshua 18.1, and remained there until the time of Samuel, 1 Samuel 14.3. However King David made **Jerusalem** the most important place in the nation and moved the ark of God to that city, 2 Samuel 6.12. His son Solomon built the temple on Mount Moriah and the people worshipped the Lord there until they were taken as prisoners to Babylon and Jerusalem was destroyed, 2 Kings 25.9.

In Deuteronomy 12 Moses told Israel to bring their offerings to the place which the Lord God would choose. Most of the offerings were eaten by the priest and the person who brought the offering. While they were in the desert they had not done it quite this way, but when they entered the land they must obey this command, **12.8-10**. The whole family of the person who brought the sacrifice could share in the feast, also any Levite who lived with him, but they must eat it only at the place which the Lord would choose, **vs.11-14**.

5/11 This does not mean that the Israelites could not eat ordinary meat in their homes if they first poured out the blood, **12.15,16**. They could eat meat at any time but they must not eat what belonged to the Lord; they must bring a tenth of what they received to the place which the Lord would choose, **vs.17,18**. In verses **19-28** Moses gave these instructions again, especially reminding the people to look after the Levites, v.19, to pour out the blood, v.23, and to bring sacrifices to the house of the Lord and also a tenth of what they received, vs.26-28.

The Israelites must not worship the false gods of the land and must destroy the places where the people had worshipped them, **12.29-32**. These nations did very wicked things and even sacrificed their own sons and daughters to their gods, v.31. The people of Israel must be careful not to follow their example.

5/12 A false prophet can sometimes prophesy correctly what will happen in the future and perform a real miracle, **13.1-4**. This is possible today and many false prophets will appear during the time of the Great Tribulation, Matthew 24.24. Satan is only a creature, but he has great power and wisdom and he can give some of his power to a man. We see that many prophets have not come from God. How can we know if a man is a false prophet? We can be sure God has not sent a prophet if he does these things in order to turn men away from following the Lord. God commanded the Israelites to kill such people, **v.5**.

God also told Israel to kill any person who tried to lead anyone to worship idols, **13.6-11**. This command shows how much God hates the worship of idols. During the present time we are not commanded to put people to death, but we can and must remain separate from those who try to turn us away from the Lord.

Israel was a holy nation, and every city was responsible to God. The people of the city must destroy anyone who worshipped an idol. If they did not do so, God commanded the other tribes to destroy the people of that city and everything in it. And they must never build it again. The Lord would be very angry with them if they did not obey these commands, **13.12-18**.

Do not follow the way of evil men, Proverbs 4.14.

Israel must be separate from other nations, chapter 14

5/13 God had promised to give Israel the land of Canaan, but the nations who lived in this land were very wicked. So were the people in neighbouring countries. God commanded Israel not to have anything to do with them when they got to Canaan.

Two of the evil customs of these people were:
1) to cut their bodies when someone died;
2) to boil a young goat in the milk of its mother.

God told Israel not to do either of these things, **14.1,21**.

Then God repeated the laws of clean and unclean animals. The Lord had given these laws to Israel about 40 years before at the beginning of their journey through the desert and we can read more details about them in Leviticus 11. The general rule for animals was the same. Two things were true about *clean* animals:
1) each foot was divided into two parts.
2) they chewed their food again after they had swallowed it, v.6; Leviticus 11.3.

In verses **4-8** Moses named ten kinds of animals which were clean and four which were unclean. The unclean animals are also listed in Leviticus 11.4-8.

The Israelites could eat only certain kinds of fish, **14.9,10**; Leviticus 11.9-12, and there were 21 different kinds of birds which they must not eat. All these birds are also listed in Leviticus 11.13-19, except one. We do not know what some of these birds are called today. Some of them, perhaps all of them, ate the flesh of dead animals. This is probably the reason why God did not allow the people of Israel to eat them. He commanded them also not to eat the meat of any animal which they had not killed but which had died of itself, **v.21**.

We do not know God's reasons for giving these rules,

but they make us think of the spiritual food of the Christian. We feed our minds with the things we read or hear and we must be careful not to feed them with anything that does not agree with God's Word. We should not receive anyone who teaches that the Lord Jesus Christ is not the eternal Son of God, 1 John 4.2,3; 2 John 9. We should not read books which deny this great truth. We must feed our souls on the Word of God and have nothing to do with the evil practices of the people around us.

5/14 God told Israel to give Him a tenth part of their crops and other things they received, **14.22**. This would also show that they were separated to God. This was not a new command, Leviticus 27.30. In Numbers 18.24 He had told them to give these tithes to the Levites for their daily food.

The Israelites had to bring the tithes of their crops and animals to a central place, eat part of them there, and give the rest to the Levites. They could also sell one tenth of their crops and bring the money to the place which God would choose. There they would buy food with part of the money and eat it before the Lord, and give the rest of the money to the Levites. The Israelites had to do this for two years, but the third year they had to stay at home and invite poor people to share the meal with them, **14.29**; Luke 14.12-14.

The Israelites obeyed some of these commands even when they were not following God any more. The prophet Amos said it was a sin for the people of Israel to do these things while their hearts were far away from God, Amos 4.4,5.

> Sometimes Christians obey God's commands so that people will think well of them, not because they want to please the Lord. The Lord looks first at our hearts, and if these are right, He is pleased when we obey Him in our actions.

The Seventh Year, chapter 15

5/15 The seventh year was the year of release, **15.1**. God had told Israel when they were at Sinai that they should make each seventh year a sabbath year, a year of rest. They and their servants had to rest during that year and they must not plow their fields so that the land could rest also, Exodus 23.11; Leviticus 25.1-7. God promised that they would have very good crops during the sixth year so that they would have enough food for the seventh year as well, Leviticus 25.18-22.

Now God told the people that they must not make other Israelites pay their debts during the seventh year. Israelites could make foreigners pay their debts to them during the year of release, **15.3**, but not another Israelite. God would bless them greatly if they obeyed His command, and there would be no poor people who needed to borrow money, **v.4**. However later in verse 11 we read that there would always be some poor people, Matthew 26.11. In the book of Psalms we often read of poor people who trusted in Jehovah, Psalm 9.18. It is the same today, John 12.8.

An Israelite could not refuse to lend money to another Israelite who was in need because the sabbatic year was near. He had to help the poor man even though he would not get his money back until the sabbatic year was over, **15.7-11**. He was also not allowed to charge high interest on the money, Leviticus 25.35-38.

5/16 Sometimes a very poor Israelite sold himself to become the slave of another Israelite. In Exodus 21.2 we read that the master had to set this slave free again after six years or during the year of *jubilee,* Leviticus 25.40. Every fiftieth year was a year of Jubilee. Now we see that the master must also give the slave some food when he set him or her free, **15.12-14**. God commanded the Israelites very plainly that they must not treat other Israelites like ordinary slaves.

Sometimes the person who served in this way preferred to go on working for his master even after the six years were over. The master would put a hole in his ear and keep him as a permanent servant, **15.16,17**; Exodus 21.5,6. This servant is a picture of the believer who serves the Lord because he loves Him and does not want anything to take him away from his Master.

How should the Christian act toward poor people? God wants us to work with our own hands as a testimony to unbelievers, 1 Thessalonians 4.11,12, and so that we might be able to give money to help people who need it, Ephesians

4.28. However if a man refuses to work, he should not eat either, 2 Thessalonians 3.10. The Lord wants us to do good to all people, especially to Christians, Galatians 6.10. Believers should help other believers who are poor, James 2.15,16; 1 John 3.17. Many people are asking for money today to help in various good activities, but Christians should use the money God has given them to help in the work of the Lord. In some countries it is impossible for a Christian to get work. In other countries a Christian might have to pay a whole week's salary for a Bible. We should try to help people like this.

Verses **19 to 23** give us more instructions about the firstborn cattle, sheep or goats, which belonged to the Lord, Exodus 13.12,13. The people should give these animals to the priests, Numbers 18.15. We now learn that the man who offered the animal would eat a holy meal with his family together with the priest at the place which the Lord would choose, v.20. However they could not give the firstborn animal to the Lord if it was lame or blind or had anything else wrong with it. They must also pour the blood of the animal on the ground. God gave these instructions because the sacrifice speaks of the Lord Jesus. It could be a picture of Him only if it was perfect in every way. The blood of the animal speaks of the death of our Lord, and the people were not allowed to use it in any way.

Three yearly feasts, 16.1-17

5/17 In this chapter Moses first reminded the people of instructions he had already given them about the Feast of Unleavened Bread, the Feast of Weeks, and the Feast of Tabernacles.

The first month of the year was called Abib. On the fourteenth day of that month the people kept the Passover, and the Feast of Unleavened Bread followed right after the Passover. For the Passover they offered a lamb for a sacrifice, **16.2**. In Numbers 28.19 we learn about the sacrifices they offered in connection with the Feast of Unleavened Bread. The people of Israel used bread baked without leaven at the time of the first Passover because they left the land of Egypt very suddenly, Exodus 12.39. This bread was also called the bread of suffering,

Deuteronomy 16.3, but it speaks of our Lord Jesus Christ who was without sin. Leaven is a picture of evil which spreads among people. There was no evil at all in the character of the Lord Jesus. God did not want any leaven to be seen in the whole country during these seven days. The people could not eat the Passover at home, but had to go to the central place which the Lord would choose, **v.6**.

In this chapter Moses did not mention the Feast of Firstfruits, Leviticus 23.10-14. The people kept the Feast of Weeks seven weeks after they began harvesting their crops. In Leviticus 23.15-21 we read about the sacrifices which they had to offer during that feast. They also had to bring an offering to the Lord, Deuteronomy **16.10**. Each person could decide what kind of an offering to bring. He could bring a large offering if the Lord had blessed him; or he could bring a small offering if he had had a lot of trouble.

Then Moses reminded the people of the Feast of Tabernacles, **16.13-15**. During the Feast of Unleavened Bread, they ate the bread of sorrow, v.3, but the Feast of Weeks was a time of joy, v.11. The Feast of Weeks was 50 days after the Feast of Firstfruits and is called Pentecost in the New Testament. During the Feast of Tabernacles also God wanted the people to rejoice, vs.14,15.

The Feast of Trumpets was on the first day of the seventh month and the Day of Atonement on the tenth, Leviticus 23.24,27. The Feast of Tabernacles began on the fifteenth day of the seventh month, Leviticus 23.34. Here in Deuteronomy Moses reminded the people of these earlier laws and insisted that all the men should appear at the place which the Lord chose three times in the year, **16.16**, and bring an offering as they were able, **v.17**.

Government, 16.18 - 17.20

5/18 The next section tells about local and national government in the land. Judges should be appointed and must judge righteously. They must be fair to all men and not accept gifts in order to show special favours to some, **16.18,19**.

The Lord told the people not to plant trees and set up idols the way the heathen people did, **16.21,22**. God hated idol worship. He was also very displeased when His people brought him sacrifices which were less than perfect. The sacrifices were pictures of Christ and only a perfect animal could represent Him properly, 17.1.

Some people think that Christ is less than God and that He could have sinned. These people are like the Israelite who brought an animal which was not perfect. God hates all such teaching because it does not bring honour to Christ.

5/19 What if anyone tried to lead others to worship idols? In 13.6-11 we saw that God commanded the people to kill such a person. Some Israelites might worship other gods, or the sun, moon, or stars. In **17.2-7** God commanded His people to judge these Israelites in the same way. A person could be put to death only if two or three witnesses agreed that he was guilty of this sin. The witnesses must throw the first stone at the guilty person, then all the people had to throw stones at him until he died, v.7.

Sometimes the elders, judges and officers in any town would not be able to decide a difficult matter. They could then go to the central place which God would choose and ask the priests and the judge to decide the matter according to the law, **17.8-13**. The people had to kill any person who refused to do what the priest or judge had decided.

Then Moses looked forward to the time when the people would ask to have a king so that they might be like the other nations around them, **17.14**. The Israelites actually did this later on; see 1 Samuel 8.5. In Deuteronomy 17 God commanded Israel not to take a man from another nation to be their king, but only the man whom He Himself would choose for them, **v.15**. The people of Israel obeyed this command for their first three kings, Saul, David, and Solomon. Then ten tribes chose Jeroboam, who led them into sin.

God did not want the king to send his servants back to Egypt to buy horses for his army, **17.16**. He also did not want him to take many wives nor to try to become very rich, **v.17**. God commanded the king to write out his own copy of the book of Deuteronomy and read it all his life, **vs.18,19**. This would help him to obey God and keep him from becoming proud, **vs.19,20**.

King David obeyed the law most of his life, but Solomon did not obey the commands of the Lord in verses 16 and 17: see 2 Chronicles 1.14-16; 1 Kings 11.1. The Lord allowed Solomon to rule over Israel for 40 years, 1 Kings 11.42, but after he died the kingdom was divided. Rehoboam, Solomon's son, ruled over part of it, and Jeroboam took the other part, 1 Kings 12.

Today God wants us to obey the rulers of our land and not set up a government of our own. He Himself has chosen a King, the Lord Jesus Christ, who will come back to rule over this earth in righteousness.

Egypt is a picture of the world and these verses teach us that we should not ask the people of the world to help us fight the battles of the Lord. We should also not give in to the lusts of the flesh nor try to become rich, because these things will draw us away from the Lord and spoil our service for Him.

The portion of the Levites, 18.1-8

5/20 God commanded Moses again to tell the people that the Levites would not receive a part of the land to live in. Instead they would receive the offerings which the other people brought to the Lord. The priest would receive the shoulder of the animal, the two cheeks and the stomach. They should also have the firstfruits of corn, wine, oil and wool. A Levite could go to the central place to serve the Lord if he wanted to do so. There he would receive part of the food offered to God, the same as the other Levites who were there.

Evil customs of the nations, 18.9-14

God told the people again that they must not have anything to do with the evil customs of other nations. They should not let people live among them who talked or listened to wicked spirits, 18.9-14. Spirits can influence men and these wicked spirits would draw people away from Jehovah. God had told the people to kill anyone who was in touch with spirits, Leviticus 20.27.

Today people or churches cannot put anyone to death for any reason. This is the work of the government which

God has given to the country. These verses teach us that God provides food for His servants (as for the Levites) and guides us in all things. We do not need to ask the spirits to tell us what we should do and it is a sin for a Christian to do so.

The coming Prophet, 18.15-22

5/21 God gave all these instructions and then made a promise about the Messiah. The Israelites had been afraid when they saw the signs of God's holiness on Mount Horeb and they asked God not so speak to them directly any more. After that God spoke to Moses and Moses passed on God's message to the people. Now God promised that He would raise up a prophet who would be like Moses, 18.18, and who would speak all that God commanded him. Therefore anyone who refused to hear the words of this Prophet would be guilty. However false prophets had to die. These prophets say that God has sent them, but they say things which He has not commanded them to say, or they speak in the name of other gods. People would know a man was a false prophet if the things which he prophesied did not happen, v.22, or if he told people not to follow the Lord any more, 13.1-5.

The New Testament tells us of the great False Prophet who will come later, the Anti-Christ. Men will receive him, but God will destroy him, John 5.43; Revelation 20.10.

The Jews asked John the Baptist if he were *the prophet.* They were thinking of the Prophet of whom Moses had spoken, John 1.21. John said he was not, and Peter said that the Lord Jesus Christ was the promised Prophet, Acts 3.19-26. Truly the Lord Jesus Christ spoke what His Father told Him to say, v.18; John 8.28. Our Lord Jesus Christ is Prophet, Priest and King and fulfils all the promises of the Old Testament. Those who refuse to obey Him refuse to obey God.

TEST YOURSELF - Deuteronomy chapters 12-18

1. Why did God choose a central place where Israel must come to worship Him?
2. Where could the Israelites eat their food?
3. How can we know if a man is a false prophet?
4. How could Israel tell if an animal was clean or not?
5. What did Israel do with 1/10 of what they received?
6. No one in Israel could work during the seventh year, the year of rest. How then could a poor man pay his debts?
7. Why would a man put a hole in his slave's ear?
8. When did the men have to go to the place the Lord was going to choose?
9. Why would God refuse a sacrifice which was not perfect?
10. Could Israel choose any man they wanted to be their king?
11. Why should we stay away from all spirits?
12. Who came and fulfilled God's promise which is found in Deuteronomy 18.18?

Turn to page 149 to check your answers.

10
END OF MOSES' SECOND MESSAGE

Cities of safety, 19.1-14

5/22 Moses had already named three cities on the west shore of the Jordan river to which people could run to save their lives, **4.41-43**. Now he reminded Israel again that they must give three cities for this purpose in the Land of Promise. They must divide the land into three parts with one of these cities in each part, **19.1-3**. They must also build roads so that the person who had killed someone by accident could run into one of these cities and save himself from his enemies. A man might be using his ax to cut wood. The head of the ax might come off and hit another person and kill him although the owner of the ax had not hated him and had not tried to hurt him. Still the dead man's brother might think he had done it on purpose and want to kill him. A man could not run to one of these cities cities to save himself if he had really planned to kill the other person, **vs.4-6**.

The Lord would give the people more land if they obeyed Him and they would have to give three more cities to which people could run for safety, **19.7-10**. God wanted to make sure that no one would die because he had accidentally killed someone. However a person might kill his neighbour because he hated him and then flee to one of these cities. The elders of that city could not allow him to stay there: they had to take him out of the city and kill him, **vs.11-13**. In Numbers 35.16-21 we read about different ways in which people try to kill others.

People often quarrel about the borders of their property and sometimes become so angry that they try to kill one another. For this reason God told the people to mark the borders of their land with stones which no one was allowed to move, **19.14**.

This is the time of God's grace, and we must not take revenge, but let the Lord Himself do it, Romans 12.19. The Lord told us not to hit a person who has hit us on the face, but to allow that person to hit the other side also, Matthew 5.39. A soldier hit the Lord too, but the Lord answered him graciously, John 18.22. He will help us to be kind and patient with those who try to make us angry.

Witnesses, 19.15-21

One person alone could not accuse another person. There had to be at least two witnesses to do so, 19.15. The priest and the judges had to judge anyone who told a lie about someone else and punish him with the same punishment that he wanted the other person to receive, v.19. The law required exact righteousness: a person who killed someone else had to be killed himself, and a person who knocked out someone's teeth had his teeth knocked out too, v.21; Exodus 21.23,24.

Moses had already told the people that there must be two or three witnesses before a murderer could be put to death, Numbers 35.30; Deuteronomy 17.6. The Lord Jesus also taught that two or three witnesses are necessary, Matthew 18.16; John 8.17; so did Paul, 2 Corinthians 13.1; 1 Timothy 5.19. People have done great harm in many churches because they heard something bad about a Christian and told others about it without first making sure that what they had heard was true.

War, chapter 20

5/23 The people of Israel would not need to be afraid when their enemies came to fight against them, even if these enemies were much stronger than they. The Lord would be with His people and the priests should tell them not to fear, **20.1-4.**

Sometimes a young Christian is afraid to talk to someone about Christ, but quite likely this person is also afraid that someone might talk to him about the Lord! We should remember that the Lord has promised to be with those who obey Him, Exodus 3.12; Matthew 28.20.

Then the officers should speak to the people and send some

men home, all those who had built a new house, planted a vineyard, or planned to be married. The officers should also send home those who were afraid because they would make others afraid too, **20.8**. The people of Israel did not have an army all the time, but all the men had to go and fight in time of war. After these people had left the captains were appointed to lead the soldiers, **v.9**.

Christians fight against wicked spirits in heavenly places, Ephesians 6.12. We must defeat sin and evil and bring sinners to Christ and we must not allow anything to keep us from fighting this spiritual battle, **20.5-7**. Christ must come before our homes, our work, and even our families, Matthew 10.37. We should love people who are not Christians even as God does, but we cannot love and share in their sins, John 3.16; 1 John 2.15.

The people of Israel might come to a distant city to fight against it. First they should offer peace to the people of the city. This meant that the people would have to pay taxes to Israel if they accepted their offer. However if they refused to make peace, the Israelites would kill all the men of the city, and the women would become servants of Israel. The Israelites could offer peace only to cities that were far away and not to those in the Land of Promise, **20.10-16**. The Lord wanted them to destroy completely the six nations mentioned in verse 17 because they were so wicked.

The Israelites must not cut down fruit trees to help them take a city, **20.19,20**. A fruit tree does not bear fruit for many years after it has been planted. The Israelites would be destroying the food of the people who would live in that city years later if they cut down these trees. So Israel had to remember to be kind and thoughtful of others even when they were fighting against their enemies.

More instructions, chapters 21,22

5/24 In chapter 19 we read about people who planned to kill someone and about those who did so by accident. Now Moses told them what they should do if they found a dead person in a field and did not know who had killed him. The elders and judges had to decide which city was nearest to the place where the body was found. Then the elders of that city had to bring a young cow which had never done any work. Someone had to take this animal to a place in the country and break its neck. Some of the priests had to go to this place too. The elders would wash their hands and say that they did not know who had killed the man, **21.1-9**. If they did know they must look for the guilty man and punish him. If they did not know, the Lord would not judge them concerning this case after the cow had been killed and they had washed their hands.

In a war the Israelites often saved the women alive and killed only the men. A man of Israel might want to marry one of these women but he had to let her live in his house for a month before he took her as his wife. He could never sell her as a slave; he must either keep her as his wife or let her go out free, **21.10-14**.

5/25 A man with two wives might love one, but hate the other. He had to give a double share of his property to his firstborn son even though he was the child of the hated wife, **21.15-17**.

God gave these commands in order to protect people who were not able to stand up for themselves, but God wants a man to have only one wife. For this reason God made only one women, Eve, for the first man, Adam. Today all over the world half the babies born are boys and half are girls, so there are about the same number of women as men. During the time of Moses many men were killed in battle and it was quite common for a man to have more than one wife. God allowed this at that time, but it was not really His will. Today it is very wrong for a man to have more than one wife.

God protected the son of the hated wife, but He commanded parents to punish the son who refused to obey, **21.18-21**. If he still refused to obey, his father and mother had to bring him before the elders of the city and the men of the city had to throw stones at him until he died. This would be very hard on the parents and they would do it only when a boy was extremely bad. It gives us an idea of how God our Father feels when His children disobey Him. He will certainly punish them to bring them back to Himself, but if they refuse, He may take them to heaven so that they will not bring shame on His Name any more.

If a person was condemned to die, people would normally kill him by throwing stones at him, 17.5. If he was hanged on a tree, they must take his body down from the tree the same day because anyone who is hanged on a tree is cursed by God, **21.23**. Paul used this verse in Galatians 3.13 to show that Christ became a curse for us. In that chapter he proved that the curse of God is on every person who does not obey God's law completely. We cannot remove this curse by doing good works or obeying God's commands, but the Lord Jesus Christ did when He died on the cross.

5/26   The first eight verses of **chapter 22** explain the command "You must love your neighbour as yourself," Luke 10.27. A man might find an animal or something else belonging to another person. He must bring it back to the owner or keep it until the owner comes to get it. God did not want a man to fool other people by wearing women's clothes, and He did not want women to fool people by wearing men's clothes, **v.5**. God did not want the Israelites to take the mother bird with the young birds or eggs, **vs.6,7**. They must let the mother go and in this way help to provide a little food for someone else also. The roof of a flat house must have a railing around it to protect the people from falling to the ground, **v.8**. These are just examples to show how God wants us to be kind and think about others.

Look out for each other's interests, not just your own,
Philippians 2.4

There were some things that the Israelites must not mix together: An ox and a donkey could not pull a plow together; people must not put two different kinds of thread into the same piece of clothing, such as wool and linen, **22.10,11**. God wanted the Israelites to put certain borders on their clothes to help them remember the things of God, **v.12**; Numbers 15.38-40.

Some of these rules may not seem important to us, but they help us to remember that we should not try to mix the things of the Lord and the things of this world. We are in the world, but we do not belong to the world, John 17.11, 14-16.

Deuteronomy 22, 23 117

5/27 The rest of chapter 22 is about marriage. A man might get married and hate his new wife. He might start talking about her and say that she was not really a pure virgin the day he married her. He would have to pay money as punishment if the parents could prove that he was telling a lie, and he could not divorce his wife. However if the wife was really guilty, she had to be put to death, **22.13-21**.

A man and a woman both had to die if they were found committing adultery. A man and a girl also had to die if she was engaged to be married to someone else, and they were caught committing sin in a city. She did not call for help and so the judges would know that she was willing to commit this sin. However only the man had to die if they were caught in the country, because no one could have heard the girl when she cried for help, **22.22-27**. Neither one would have to die if the girl was not engaged to another man; instead the man must pay the girl's father and they had to get married, **vs.28,29**. A man must not have sexual relations with his father's wife. If he did, both of them had to die, Leviticus 20.11.

These verses teach us that God hates sin between men and women. Many Christians live among people who think these things are not important. Let us remember that we have been cleansed from our sins and set apart for God and have received the Holy Spirit of God, 1 Corinthians 6.9-11.

Holiness in the camp, 23.1-14

5/28 Some Israelites could not worship like regular members of the nation, for example, a man who could not have any children because part of his body had been cut off; or a person whose parents had not been married, **23.1,2**.

The Israelites could not receive among them the Ammonites and the Moabites, the descendants of Lot, even after ten generations, Genesis 19.37,38. These people had refused to help Israel and had hired the prophet Balaam to curse them. The Lord had turned this curse into a blessing, Numbers 23.11, but those who tried to curse were still guilty, **23.3-6**. Later on we see that God's grace was greater than His law and Ruth the Moabitess was accepted among the people of Israel as the wife of Boaz.

In the same way God's curse is on all who break the law, but because Christ died we can by grace come into God's family forever.

The grandchildren of an Edomite or an Egyptian also could not worship with the people of God, but their children could be accepted, **23.7,8**.

In time of war the Israelites had to be especially careful to keep themselves clean, **23.9**. A person might become unclean by accident; he would have to stay outside the camp until evening, **vs.10,11**. God was with His people in the camp. This fact explains the good health rule in verses **12-14**.

Believers are fighting all the time against wicked spiritual forces and the Lord is always with us. For these reasons we should keep ourselves from everything that is unclean.

5/29 In the rest of the chapter there are various rules about showing kindness and what to do concerning different matters. A slave who ran away from his master could live safely with any Israelite who had to treat him kindly, **23.15,16**. We have an example of this in the New Testament. Onesimus ran away from his master but Paul led him to Christ. Paul asked him to return to his master Philemon. Philemon was also a Christian and would treat Onesimus as a brother in the Lord, Philemon 16.

God did not allow any sexual sin between two men or between two women, **23.17,18**; Romans 1.26,27. Some people in Judah were guilty of these things later on, 1 Kings 14.24, but King Asa removed them, 1 Kings 15.12. Later King Jehoshaphat had to do the same thing, 1 Kings 22.46. There are very strong commands in the New Testament telling us not to do these things.

An Israelite might lend money to another Israelite but could not ask him to pay interest on the money that he had borrowed, **23.19,20**. He must do everything he promised God of his own free will, **vs.21-23**. He could eat grapes in his neighbour's vineyard when he was hungry, or pick corn in his neighbour's field, but he could not take anything away with him to eat later on, vs.**24,25**.

These verses show us that God is interested in every detail of our lives in this world.

God bought you for a price. So use your bodies for God's glory.
1 Corinthians 6.20

Justice and mercy, chapters 24 and 25

5/30 Moses' law allowed a man to divorce his wife by giving her a letter. She could then marry another man, but she could not return to her first husband even if she was divorced again or if her second husband died, **24.1-4**. A man did not have to go to war for one year after he was married, nor do any other work for the nation, so that he might be free to care for his new wife, **v.5**.

Today many worldly people become divorced, but this is not God's will except when the other person has been unfaithful, Matthew 19.3-9. Here again God's people should not follow the example of the people of the world. God hates divorce, Malachi 2.16.

A person had to be killed if he was caught stealing an Israelite in order to sell him as a slave, **24.7**. Today very few people are slaves of others, but the Lord Jesus taught that everyone who sins is a slave of sin, John 8.34. God will certainly judge those who lead others into sin by their teaching or by their example. He will surely punish people who become rich by encouraging others to sin.

In Leviticus 13 and 14 the Lord gave rules for those who had leprosy. Even Miriam had to stay outside the camp for a week after she was cured, **24.8,9**; Numbers 12.14.

The Israelites should show mercy to poor people and treat them fairly. A person who borrows money might give something else as pledge that he will pay back the money later on. At that time the lender would return the pledge. However the lender could not take the other person's *mill stone* which he used to grind his grain, **24.6**, for this would make it impossible for the person to earn money for his needs. The lender was not allowed to go into the man's house to get the pledge, but had to wait until the man brought it out to him. If a man gave his clothes as a pledge, the lender must give them back to him the same day, **vs.10-13**. A lender could not take a widow's clothing as a pledge, **v.17**.

6/1 A man had to pay his workmen on the day their wages were due, **24.14,15**.

The New Testament also teaches that masters should treat their workmen fairly, James 5.4. There would be far fewer problems between employers and workmen if people would obey these commands in the Bible. However our work as Christians is not to try and improve conditions of workmen, but to preach the Gospel to them and to all men.

God will judge every person for his own sins, **24.16**. For example, Korah rebelled against God and died very suddenly, but his children did not die with him, Numbers 16.33; 26.11.

God wanted the Israelites to treat foreigners and orphans fairly, **24.17**, and to allow poor people to gather grain, olives and grapes after the harvest workers were finished. The reapers should even leave a little in the fields for the poor people, **vs.19-21**. Boaz told his workmen to do this, Ruth 2.15,16. The Israelites had been slaves in Egypt, but God had set them free, **vs.18,22**, and so they should be fair and kind to others.

This is also true of us and we understand that we should live for Christ because He died for us, 2 Corinthians 5.15. He set us free so that we are no longer slaves of sin.

Chapter 25

6/2 The judges had to judge righteously when men brought their quarrels to them. The judge might say that one of the men deserved to be beaten with a whip. The judge himself had to watch while the man was punished, but he could not order the man to receive more than 40 lashes, **25.1-3**. The Jewish judges thought that Paul was a wicked man because he served the Lord Jesus Christ. He received 39 lashes on five different occasions up to the time he wrote 2 Corinthians 11.24, and perhaps more later.

God wanted the people to be kind to animals, **25.4**. They should allow an ox to eat while he is treading out the grain. Paul used this verse to show that the Lord's people should look after

Deuteronomy 24-26

the needs of those who preach the Gospel, 1 Corinthians 9.9; 1 Timothy 5.18.

Sometimes a married man died before he had any children. The man's brother should then marry his widow, and her first child would have the same name as the dead brother, **25.5,6**. However perhaps the brother of the dead man did not want to marry the widow. He would have to tell the elders of the city about this. Then the widow had the right to insult him in front of everybody, **vs.8-10**.

One day the Sadducees tried to make the Lord Jesus say something wrong. They mentioned this law and told a story about seven brothers who all took the same wife one after another but she had no children. Then they asked who would be the woman's husband when the dead were raised to life. The Sadducees themselves did not believe in the resurrection and thought it was foolish to teach that the dead would be raised to life. The Lord Jesus told them they were wrong because they did not know the Scriptures nor God's power, Matthew 22.23-33.

How foolish for anyone to think that he is wiser than the Lord Jesus Christ or able to win in an argument with God!

Two men might fight together and the wife of one of them might try to help her husband by injuring the private parts of the body of the other. This was very serious and the people were to punish her by cutting off her hand, **25.11,12**.

Verses **13-16** remind us again of the law of honest weights and measures. See Leviticus 19.35,36.

These laws taught the Israelites that they should act righteously toward each other and be merciful to one another. Then Moses commanded the Israelites to punish the Amalekites because the Amalekites had fought against them in the desert right after the Israelites left Egypt, **25.17-19**; Exodus 17.8-16. Later during the time of Saul and Samuel the Israelites did destroy the Amalekites, 1 Samuel 15.1-3.

The end of Moses' second message, chapter 26

6/3 Moses had given the Israelites many laws and rules, but at the end of his second message he taught them more about how to worship the Lord.

First he reminded them of the law of firstfruits. God had commanded His people to give to Him the firstfruits of their harvest, Exodus 23.19; 34.26 and Numbers 15.20 and 18.13. In Leviticus 23.10-14 and Deuteronomy 16.9-11 we read about the Feast of Firstfruits.

Now Moses told the people that they should bring a basket full of the firstfruits of their fields to the central place which the Lord would choose. They should take it to the priest and declare that the Lord had brought them into the Land of Promise, **26.1-3.** They should remember how good the Lord had been to the people of Israel from the time when Jacob went down to Egypt to the time when the Lord delivered them out of Egypt and brought them into the Land of Promise. Their hearts would be filled with joy and worship as they brought their firstfruits to the Lord and thought about all His goodness to them, **vs.10,11.**

In the third year the Israelites had to give one tenth of all food grown in their fields to the priest and to poor people. When they had done this they would be able to tell the Lord that they had obeyed His command, and ask Him to bless their nation, **26.12-15.**

> We too must obey the Lord if we want Him to bless us. For example it is useless for a Christian to ask the Lord to guide him if he is not obeying what the Lord has already commanded him in His Word.

The people had agreed that Jehovah was their God and had promised that they would obey His commands, **26.17.** At the same time God said that they would be His special nation, closer to Him than other nations, **vs.18,19.** We too are called God's own people and should praise Him and proclaim His wonderful acts, 1 Peter 2.9.

Moses' second message was quite long, from chapter 5 to chapter 26, the largest part of the book of Deuteronomy. In it he repeated the Ten Commandments and gave many detailed instructions about commands and regulations which he had given earlier. The book of Deuteronomy shows us the spiritual meaning of

God's commands more than the books of Exodus, Leviticus and Numbers, and so is more closely connected with the New Testament. Today we are not under law, but under grace, but we will find many helpful, spiritual lessons for our own lives if we read these messages in Deuteronomy carefully.

TEST YOURSELF - Deuteronomy chapters 19-26

1. What would be done to a man who lied about another person?
2. Who were to be sent home from the battle?
3. What should the people do if they found a dead man and did not know who killed him?
4. How does God the Father feel when His children disobey Him?
5. What can we learn from the rules given in Deuteronomy 22.9-12?
6. Why was sin in the city worse than sin in the country?
7. God's law said no Moabite could become a member of the nation of Israel. How then could Israel receive Ruth as a member?
8. Why did Paul ask Onesimus to return to his master Philemon?
9. Does the Bible allow Christians to get a divorce?
10. Why did God tell the people of Israel to leave a little grain and fruit for poor people?
11. What is the main lesson for us in Deuteronomy chapters 24 and 25?
12. Exodus, Leviticus, Numbers and Deuteronomy all contain God's commands to His people. How is Deuteronomy different from the others?

Turn to page 150 to check your answers.

11
Moses' Third Message and Last Words

Moses' third message is quite short, like his first one. In chapters 27 and 28 we see Moses standing with the elders of Israel, 27.1, and with the priests, 27.9. Together they told the people of Israel why God would bless the people or curse them. In chapters 29 and 30 God made another covenant with Israel, 29.1.

6/4 Moses, together with the elders, first commanded the people to set up great stones on Mount Ebal, cover them with plaster, and write on them the words of the law. Mount Ebal was the mountain of the curse, **27.13**, and the Law brought a curse. But in addition to the stones of the law, Moses also told the people to build an *altar* there, **v.5**. They were to make this altar of whole stones which had not been shaped with any tool. On this altar they were to offer whole burnt offerings and peace offerings. The burnt offerings speak of our Lord Jesus Christ who was completely set apart to God and obeyed Him perfectly. The peace offerings also speak of Christ. We can enjoy peace and fellowship with God because the Lord Jesus Christ died on the cross for us. So the stones of the law on the mountain of the curse could not condemn the people because the altar of the Lord was there also.

Together with the priests Moses told the Israelites that they were the people of Jehovah and must obey His commands, **27.9,10**.

6/5 Mount Ebal and Mount Gerizim were in the central part of the land of Israel. We have already read a little about them in 11.29. Now Moses told six of the tribes to stand on Mount Gerizim and six on Mount Ebal. Those on Mount Gerizim were to tell of blessing.

Mount Gerizim	Mount Ebal
the blessing	*the curse*
Simeon	Reuben
Levi	Gad
Judah	Asher
Issachar	Zebulun
Joseph	Dan
Benjamin	Naphthali

Moses told the Levites to stand on Mount Gerizim, the place of blessing, and to declare twelve curses with a loud voice, **27.14-26**. All the people would say **Amen** to show that they agreed with the judgment of the Lord. The following people would be cursed:

Those who worship idols, v.15.

Those who do not honour their parents, v.16.

Those who act unrighteously, vs.17-19.

Those who commit adultery, vs.20-23.

Those who strike and kill other people, vs.24,25.

All who do not obey the whole law, v.26.

Verse 26 gives us in short form the main teaching of chapter 27. The Holy Spirit used this verse in Galatians 3.10 to prove that all who try to keep the law are under God's curse unless they obey every command.

Moses told the people to write the law on great stones on Mount Ebal, the mountain of the curse. The Levites stood on Mount Gerizim to "bless", but Moses told them to pronounce twelve curses. The law could only curse those who tried to keep it, but God blesses His people because He is gracious.

6/6   God promised to bless the people of Israel **if** they obeyed His commands, **28.1-14**. Notice the word "if" in verses 1 and 9. In verses 3-6 we see six blessings; these are all for this world.

The Lord Jesus gave ten blessings or beatitudes when He told about the kingdom of heaven in Matthew 5.3-12. God the Father has blessed us with every spiritual gift through

Christ, Ephesians 1.3. The book of Revelation tells us of seven more blessings; see 1.3; 14.13; 16.15; 19.9; 20.6; 22.7,14.

If Israel obeyed, the Lord would do seven things for them:
1. give them victory over their enemies, v.7;
2. give them good crops, v.8;
3. set them up as a holy people, v.9;
4. call them His very own people, v.10;
5. give them large families, many cattle, and fruitful fields, v.11;
6. give them plenty of rain, v.12;
7. give them great honour among the other nations, v.13.

6/7 These are wonderful blessings, but God knew that the people would disobey, and in the rest of this long chapter He told them what would happen when they disobeyed. The blessings in verses 3 to 6 would all be changed to curses, **28.16-19**. The Lord would send them sickness, **vs.21,27,28,35**. There would be no rain, **v.24**. The locusts would eat up their crops so that there would be famine, **vs.38-40**; other nations would cause them trouble and take their property, **vs.30-34**. Their enemies would defeat them, **vs.25, 26,43**; and take them to distant lands as prisoners, **vs.36,41**.

6/8 Their enemy would be a fierce nation from a great distance, **28.49**. The soldiers of this nation would surround Israel and stop them from getting any food. The people would become so hungry they would have to eat human flesh, even their own children, **vs.53-57**.

6/9 There would also be terrible diseases, **28.58-62**. The people would be taken to many other countries as prisoners, **vs.63,64**, but even in these lands they would not be able to live in peace; they would always be afraid of what might happen to them, **vs.65-67**. Some would even go back to Egypt as slaves, **v.68**.

The people of Israel had many opportunities to know and obey God and it seems hard to believe that they would actually have to suffer these things. However in 2 Kings and 2 Chronicles we see that the Lord's warnings in this chapter were all fulfilled.

In this present time God has given believers wonderful

promises and many opportunities to serve Him, but even so the Church is getting further and further away from Him. We can read about this in Revelation 2 and 3. There we see the Lord Jesus Christ has risen from death and is now examining the seven churches and has to judge most of them. Finally He says to Laodicea, *I am about to spit you out of my mouth!* Revelation 3.16.

The third covenant of the law, chapters 29, 30

6/10   God first gave the law in Exodus 20-23. He promised that Israel would be a kingdom of priests and a holy nation if they obeyed, Exodus 19.5,6. The people agreed to do everything the Lord had commanded, Exodus 19.8; 24.7,8. In these chapters we do not read that a person could be forgiven if he disobeyed any part of the law, so we can call this the covenant of **pure law**.

Then God told Moses to climb to the top of Mount Sinai again, Exodus 24.12. This time He told Moses that the people should make the Tabernacle, Exodus 25-31. God also gave Moses two pieces of stone on which He had written the law with His own finger, 31.18. Of course God knew in advance that the people would not keep His commands, and He provided the Tabernacle so that He could forgive them when they sinned. They could come to the door of the Tabernacle and the priest could represent them before God by going into the Tabernacle where God dwelt. After they had built the Tabernacle God told them what sacrifices they should offer to Him, Leviticus 1-7. We can call this arrangement the **Sinaitic covenant**, Exodus 34.10,27,28. It was a covenant of law mixed with mercy so that God would be able to forgive those who disobeyed Him.

Now in Deuteronomy 29 and 30 God told Moses to make another covenant with the Israelites. We can call this the **Deuteronomic covenant**. First Moses reminded them how God delivered them from Egypt and protected and cared for them in the desert and helped them to defeat their enemies, **29.2-9**. Still many Israelites did not really believe, even though they had seen all these signs and miracles, v.4; Amos 5.25,26.

Does this seem hard to understand? Remember that today millions of people have grown up in so-called Christian lands, yet many of them do not really believe in Christ. Are we any better than Israel?

6/11 But even if they did not believe they were still under the covenant of the law. Moses showed plainly that this covenant was for all the Israelites and the foreigners who lived among them, those who were there at the time and those who were away, **29.11,15**. The people of Israel had lived in the land of Egypt and as they travelled to the land of Canaan they had also seen other nations worship idols, **vs.16,17**. The Lord would certainly judge any man or woman, any family or tribe who stopped following the Lord and worshipped idols, **vs.18-20**. These people would be like a bitter plant that causes trouble among the other people.

Today also some Christians do not truly follow the Lord, and they can cause trouble and quarreling among the believers, Hebrews 12.15.

The Lord would judge these people, but their bad example would turn others away from the Lord also. God would have to judge them too until finally the whole land would become so bad that people could not live in it, **29.22,23**. People of other nations would ask why the Lord had done this. They would be told it was because Israel had not kept the covenant which the Lord had made with them, **vs.24,25**. God has not revealed everything to us, but we must pay attention to the many things which He has shown us in the Scriptures, **v.29**. Moses was a prophet and God showed him that the people of Israel would sin. Then their enemies would make them prisoners and take them away to another land. We will read more about this in chapters 31 and 32.

6/12 In **30.1-10** Moses told the people that they would be prisoners in another country, and also that they would come back to their own land. God would bring them back if they turned to Him in their trouble, vs.1-3. Nebuchadnezzar, king of Babylon, took the people of Israel as prisoners to his country, 2 Kings 25, but in Ezra 1 we see that some of them returned to their own land.

The Lord Jesus said that Jerusalem would be destroyed again because the people of Israel did not accept Him as their Messiah, Luke 21.6. This took place in the year 70 A.D., about 40 years after the Lord Jesus Christ was crucified. In the last days the people of Israel will come back to their land, but they will still not believe that Christ is their Messiah.

Even now thousands of Jews from all over the world have returned to the land of Israel and this makes us think that the Lord Jesus will return soon. We too should be ready because we do not know just when He will come, Luke 12.40.

Moses promised that the Lord would bless the people after He had brought them back even more than He had before, 30.5,6. He would use some nations to punish His people Israel, but He would punish these nations with the same punishment, v.7. God had used the nation of Babylon to punish Israel, but the Babylonians were so cruel that they did much more than what God had commanded them to do, and God said He would destroy them, Isaiah 13.19.

God had told Israel plainly what He wanted them to do. No one would have to go to heaven or to some distant land to find out what God's will was. Moses had given God's commands to them and he was right there among them, **30.11-14**.

The apostle Paul used words like these when he wrote about the Gospel in Romans 10.6-9. The Gospel is for all the people of the world, but no one can believe it until he has heard it. That is why we must send people to preach the Gospel to people in other lands, Romans 10.14,15.

God was making this covenant of the law with Israel and it was also very simple: If they obeyed, God would bless them, **30.16**. If they disobeyed, He would punish them, **vs.17,18**. So they had to choose if they wanted the blessing of the Lord, and life, or if they wanted God's curse, and death, **vs.15,19**.

Moses' last words, chapters 31-33

6/13 Moses finished his third message by telling the Israelites plainly about God's covenant with them. In chapter 31 Moses gave his last instructions to Israel. In chapter 32 he sang a song of praise about Jehovah, and in chapter 33 he blessed all the tribes of Israel.

Moses' last instructions to Israel, chapter 31

Moses lived 40 years in Pharaoh's house, Acts 7.22,23, and was 80 years old when God brought the people of Israel out of Egypt, Exodus 7.7. During the last 40 years of his life he had travelled through the desert with the people of Israel and now he was 120 years old, **31.2**. His mind and body were still strong, 34.7, but he could not lead Israel any more because the Lord had told him that he would not cross the Jordan river. Moses knew that he would die soon and so he encouraged the people to be strong and brave because God would not fail them, **v.6**.

Then Moses called Joshua and told him to be strong also, and not to be afraid, because Jehovah was with him, **31.7,8**.

Probably Joshua did not feel very brave even after Moses had spoken to him, but God gave him the courage later when he needed it. The time came for him to lead the armies of Israel to fight against their enemies and then Joshua was brave.

> God always gives us the strength to do difficult things for Him. He gives this at the time when He wants us to do them, but not before.

Moses left the people of Israel with a leader to take his place after he died, and he also left them the law of God. He commanded the priests to read the law to the people of Israel every seven years at the Feast of Tabernacles. This was so that they would not forget it and so that their children would learn the ways of the Lord, **31.10-13**.

6/14 Then the Lord called Moses and Joshua and spoke to them at the door of the Tabernacle. He told them that the people would begin to worship idols after Moses had died. Then the Lord gave Moses a song which would remind the people later on that God had made a covenant with them, **31.14-21**. The Lord also promised to be with Joshua, **v.23**. When Moses had finished writing the law in a book he told the priests to put it into the ark to keep it safe, **vs.9,25,26**. Then he told the elders and the officers to come near while he told the words of his song to the whole nation, **vs.28-30**.

Moses' song, chapter 32

6/15 We do not have the music for Moses' song, but in the Hebrew Bible this chapter is written like a song. Moses also wrote Psalm 90 and some Bible students think the Holy Spirit led him to write Psalm 91 as well.

In this song Moses repeated many of the things which he had already taught the people in his three messages, but probably the people would remember them better in the form of a song and repeat them more often. Some of the sentences in this song are hard to understand, but the main teaching is very clear. In this song Moses sometimes called the people of Israel "he" or "they" and sometimes he talked to them and said "you".

In the first two verses Moses called on those in heaven and on earth to listen to him. God is great, strong, perfect and righteous, **32.3,4**. The people had sinned and had not acted as children of God should, **vs.5,6**. Moses told them to remember how God had delivered them again and again, **vs.7-14**. God had thought of Israel when He divided the earth among all people years before Israel was even a nation, v.8. He cared for them in the desert, vs.10-12, and provided plenty of the best food for them in the land of Canaan, vs.13,14. All these things showed how much God loved His people.

6/16 Jeshurun is another name for Israel, **32.15**, Isaiah 44.2. The people would forget God when everything went well with them and start to worship demons, **vs.16,17**. When they left the Lord, v.15, He would hide Himself from them, v.20.

God would punish them according to the measure of their sin. He had promised that He would be their God and they would be His people, but He would use another nation to punish them if they broke His covenant and started to worship false gods, .**32.21**; Hosea 1.9. God's anger will kindle a fire, **v.22**, which will later destroy this earth, 2 Peter 3.10,12, and burn forever in the lake of fire, Revelation 20.10. God would punish the nation of Israel severely and they would have to suffer terrible things, but He would not destroy them completely, **vs.21-27**. If He did Satan and his servants would say that they had destroyed Israel and not the Lord, v.27.

The nation God used to punish His people knew nothing about God and His ways, **32.28,29**, but they would defeat Israel easily because God would help them to do so, **v.30**. This nation did not worship Jehovah but were very cruel, **vs.31-33**. God will remember this when He judges the nations, **vs.34-36**.

6/17 Finally the people of Israel would understand that they were very weak and that the gods whom they worshipped were weak too, **32.37,38**. At that time God would help them. He is over all nations and controls the whole world, **vs.39-42**, and He will defeat all His enemies. The old Hebrew Bible says in verse **43** that God will call on the nations to rejoice when He takes revenge on the enemies of Israel, Romans 15.10. The nation which punished Israel would cause other nations to suffer too. These nations will be glad when Jehovah destroys His enemies, v.43.

6/18 Moses and Joshua gave this song to the people and Moses warned them again that they should obey, **32.44-47**.

That day Jehovah reminded Moses that he would soon die. He told Moses to climb Mount Abarim (also called Nebo), **32.48-52**. From the top of this mountain God would let him see the land of Canaan before he died. The people of Israel sinned when they camped at Kadesh-barnea the first time, and they all died in the desert. Moses sinned when Israel came back to Kadesh-barnea and he too had to die before the nation entered Canaan, the land God had promised to give them. Many years later Moses and Elijah appeared to the Lord Jesus when He was with Peter, James and John on a mountain in Canaan, Matthew 17.3.

These things show us that God is both kind and severe, Romans 11.22. We can see again and again how kind He was to Moses and all Israel and how much He loved them. Moses reminded the people of this in these chapters. However God had to punish them, and even Moses, when they sinned. He would bring them into the land of Canaan because He was kind and loving, but if they sinned, He would punish them because He is righteous. Then, if they repented, He would kindly bring them back to Himself.

Moses blessed the tribes, chapter 33

6/19 In chapter 32 Moses had prophesied that the people of Israel would depart from the Lord and that God would have to judge them. He did not prophesy these things because he hated the people. In 9.26 and Numbers 14.13-19 we can see how much he loved them by the way he prayed for them. Now in chapter 33 the Holy Spirit led him to bless the tribes of Israel before he died. This chapter is also written like a song and some parts are hard to understand. Moses was a prophet and the Holy Spirit led him to prophesy these things which happened later on.

First Moses reminded the people that the Lord came to Sinai to give the law, **33.1-5**. The "holy ones" in verse 2 may be angels, Acts 7.53; Galatians 3.19. Why did God give the covenant of the law to His people? Because He loved them, v.3. This is the reason for everything He does to or for men. Moses gave God's law to the people but Jehovah was really the King in Jeshurun (Israel), vs.4,5.

Jacob also blessed the twelve tribes before he died, Genesis 49. He blessed Leah's sons first, then the sons of Leah's slave-girl and the sons of Rachel's slave-girl, and finally the sons of Rachel. In Deuteronomy 33 Moses also blessed the sons of Leah first, then the sons of Rachel, and then the others. We do not read of a blessing for Simeon in this chapter, but we do not know the reason for this.

6/20 1. **Reuben.** Moses prayed that the tribe of Reuben would continue to exist, **33.6**. Dathan and Abiram were of the tribe of Reuben and had died when Korah rebelled against the Lord, Numbers 16.1,27,31-33, but the tribe of Reuben would continue even though some of the men of the tribe had committed such terrible sin.

2. **Judah.** Jacob showed that the future king of Israel would be a man of the tribe of Judah, Genesis 49.10. Now Moses prayed that the Lord would hear when Judah cried to Him, and help him to defeat his enemies, **33.7**.

3. **Levi.** The tribe of Levi was especially near to Jehovah during the period of the law. God gave Levi *the Urim and the Thummin,* **33.8**. These precious stones helped the high priest to

find out the will of God, Exodus 28.30. They were part of the breast piece and ephod which he wore.

God had tested or proved Moses and Aaron, both Levites, at Massah and Meribah, Exodus 17.7. God tested Phinehas, Aaron's grandson; he showed that he was on God's side when he killed Zimri of the tribe of Simeon. This was to punish him for sinning with a Midianite woman in front of all the people, Numbers 25.6-8,14. Phinehas did not "acknowledge" his brothers, **v.9**; this means that he punished wicked men even though they belonged to his own nation. In the same way the Levites obeyed God when they punished the Israelites who worshipped the gold calf, Exodus 32.26-29. The work of the tribe of Levi was to teach the people of Israel and to offer sacrifices to God, **v.10**. Moses prayed that God would accept the work of the Levites and protect them from their enemies, **v.11**.

4. **Benjamin.** Moses said that God would love Benjamin and protect him, **33.12**.

6/21 5. **Joseph** followed the Lord more closely than all the other sons of Jacob. Moses prayed that God might bless Joseph's land and all the precious things in it, **33.13-16**. Joseph was like a Nazirite, separate from his brothers, **v.16**, Genesis 49.26. The tribe of Ephraim would be greater than the tribe of Manasseh, **v.17**, Genesis 48.20, and was the leading tribe until David became king. Joshua belonged to the tribe of Ephraim, Numbers 13.8, and this tribe lived in the center of the country.

6/22 6 and 7. **Zebulun and Issachar.** The tribe of Zebulun lived by the sea, Genesis 49.13, and Moses' blessing on these two tribes seems to be for them as they bought and sold to other nations, **33.18,19**.

8. **Gad** was one of the tribes which chose to live on the east side of Jordan. They came across Jordan to help the people of Israel possess the land of Canaan, **33.20,21**.

9. **Dan.** The tribe of Dan led the other tribes to depart from the Lord, Judges 18.30, and it is not mentioned with the other tribes in Revelation 7.

10. **Naphthali** would be satisfied with the blessing of the

Lord. Their land was to the west and south of the Sea of Galilee, **33.23**.

6/23 11. **Asher**. The word Asher means happy or blessed. Moses prayed that this tribe would have many children and that it might be the favourite of the other tribes.

God gives His people the strength they need day by day, **33.25**. This promise is for us also. The Lord will give us new strength as we come to Him in prayer, Isaiah 40.31, and God's power is strongest when we know that we are very weak, 2 Corinthians 12.9.

In the last few verses of the chapter Moses spoke to the whole nation. There was no god like their God, **33.26**. He rides in the heavens to help His people. The people of God would live in safety if they were separate from the world, **v.28**. They would be happy and different from all other peoples. The Lord would guard them and defeat their enemies, **v.29**.

Only in heaven will we find out how wonderfully God has cared for us in this world. Let us praise Him even now as He leads us day by day.

Jehovah wanted the nation of Israel to be His servant, but they failed. However in these blessings we can see pictures of the perfect Servant of Jehovah, the Lord Jesus Christ.

The name Reuben means "See, a Son", Genesis 29.32. We can see the Son of God in the blessing of Reuben. He would live and not die. The Lord Jesus will never die again and God wants us to look to Him, Matthew 12.18; Hebrews 12.2.

In the blessing of Judah we can see a picture of Christ's present work; He is praying for His people, Hebrews 7.25, and we know that God hears the voice of His Son. God will also help Christ defeat His enemies, Psalm 110.1.

The blessing of Levi reminds us of the temptation of the Lord Jesus Christ. He also put the work of God first, Luke 2.49; Matthew 12.48. His work was to teach people the ways of God and His whole life and His death were like a sacrifice of a sweet smell to God, a whole burnt offering, Ephesians 5.2. Moses prayed that God might accept the work of Levi, v.11. God raised the Lord Jesus Christ from death to prove that God accepted Him and His work. All men will see this when Christ comes back to rule in power and to defeat all His enemies.

Benjamin means "the son of my right hand"; the right hand is the place of power and nearness, Genesis 35.18. The Son of God was always at the Father's side, John 1.18. In John's gospel we read seven times that God the Father loves His Son, and in Acts 7.55,56 Stephen saw Christ at God's right hand.

Like Joseph the Lord Jesus Christ was separate from His brothers. He grew up in Nazareth and lived in Israel, but His perfect life was very different from the lives of the people around Him. Joseph received glory and the power to rule in Egypt and the Lord Jesus will be glorified and rule over this world with power, v.17.

In general the blessing of Moses looks forward to the time of the Millennium when Israel will be the most important nation of the world. At that time God will show His love for Israel and all nations, v.3. He will defeat Israel's enemies and greatly bless that nation, vs.7,11,17,20,29.

At the same time the Church will be still closer to the King of kings, the Lord Jesus Christ. Let us be careful that we do not bring dishonour on His name while people still refuse to accept Him as their Saviour and Lord.

Moses died and was buried, chapter 34

6/24   Moses finished blessing the tribes and the whole nation and then he climbed Mount Nebo. From the top of the mountain God let him see the land which He had promised to give to the descendants of Abraham, Isaac and Jacob, **34.1-4**. Moses died there on the mountain and the Lord Himself buried him. The people would probably have started to worship at Moses' grave if they had known where it was.

We do not know who wrote about Moses' death in chapter 34. Moses was a prophet and perhaps the Holy Spirit led him to write about his own death. It is more likely that Joshua wrote this chapter, but we do not really need to know. We do not know the authour of some of the psalms and other parts of the Old Testament, but we can be sure that the Holy Spirit led all the writers of the 66 books of the Bible in everything they wrote.

When Moses died at the age of 120 years his body and mind were still strong. The people of Israel grieved for him for 30 days as they had done for Aaron. The Egyptians had grieved 70 days for Jacob when he died, Genesis 50.3. When the greatest Man in the Bible died, His disciples grieved for Him for only three days. Then, praise the Lord, He rose again from death!

TEST YOURSELF - Deuteronomy chapters 27-34
1. Why did the Levites stand on the mount of blessing and declare only curses?
2. Why did God command Israel to build an altar on Mount Ebal?
3. Why are there more curses than blessings in chapter 27?
4. Which books in the Bible show that these terrible things really came on Israel?
5. Was the Deuteronomic covenant based on God's mercy?
6. Where would Israel have to go to find God's Law?
7. What are the three parts of Moses' life?
8. What other song did Moses write, besides Deuteronomy 32?
9. Who were Jacob and Jeshurun mentioned in 32.15?
10. Why did God keep Moses and many Israelites from entering the land of Canaan?
11. How did some Levites prove that they wanted to follow the Lord?
12. How many tribes did Moses bless in chapter 33?
13. What verses about Christ remind us of the blessing on Benjamin?
14. Who wrote Deuteronomy 34?

Turn to page 150 to check your answers.

The Teaching of Deuteronomy   12

It is necessary to think if you wish to learn. This part of your book will help you to learn what Deuteronomy teaches about God, about Christ and about our salvation. Here is how you do it.

Take a card or a piece of paper and cover all this page except the part you are reading now. Move the card down slowly a little at a time so you can read some more. After Frame 1 you will see a question. Think about this question and try to answer it. Then move your card down until you can read the answer. If you got the right answer, go on to the next paragraph. If your answer was wrong, go back and read again the whole paragraph, then try again.

6/25 1. The Bible claims that God has revealed Himself in it, and the book of Deuteronomy is the same. Who gave Moses the commands which he repeated to Israel, 1.3? _____

_____

God did.
==
2. God is true, 32.4, and He has revealed to man *all things* or *many things* or *nothing* (choose the right answer), 29.29. _____

_____

Many things.
==
3. Where must men go to get these commands, to heaven or across the sea, 30.11-14? _____

_____

We do not have to go far away because these commands are very near.
==
6/26 4. The Lord Jesus quoted from three verses in Deuteronomy, 6.13; 6.16; 8.3. What does this prove about the book of Deuteronomy? _____

_____

He believed that it is the Word of God.

From these verses we can say that God spoke through Moses and that Deuteronomy is part of the Word of God.
==
5. Now let us think of what Deuteronomy teaches about God Himself.

The Teaching of Deuteronomy

No man has seen God in all His glory, 4.15, but the Bible tells us what He is like and how He always acts. There are several words which describe God's character; these words are called *attributes*. Most of the attributes of God can be learned from Deuteronomy. For example,

    God is eternal
    He has all power
    He is over all
    He knows everything.

These are four of the attributes of God. Now read the verses given and write in the attribute of God which each verse teaches:

1. Deuteronomy 31.21   I know....their thoughts _____
2. Deuteronomy 32.40   I live forever _____
3. Deuteronomy 4.39 _____
4. Deuteronomy 8:16 _____
5. Deuteronomy 10.17 _____
6. Deuteronomy 29.29 _____
7. Deuteronomy 32.8 _____

----

1. God knows men's thoughts and all future events, He knows all, 31.21.
2. God lives forever, He is eternal, 32.40.
3. The Lord is in heaven, He is supreme over all, 4.39.
4. He fed the people in the desert, He has all power, 8.16.
5. He is God of gods and Lord of lords, He is over all, 10.17.
6. Hidden things belong to God, He knows everything, 29.29.
7. God is the Most High, He laid the boundaries for all nations. He is above all, 32.8.

==

6. Here is another thing about God: God is Light, He reveals Himself, 1 John 1.5. Also God is faithful, He never changes, James 1.17. Which of these verses in Deuteronomy teaches that God reveals Himself? Which teaches that He is always faithful?

    1. Deuteronomy 4.36 _____
    2. Deuteronomy 7.9 _____

----

    1. God spoke from heaven to instruct the people, He reveals Himself to men, 4.36.
    2. He is faithful and keeps His covenant, 7.9.

==

140 Desert Journey

6/27 **7.** God is also righteous, 32.4, and merciful, 4.31. He loved the people of Israel, 7.8,13, and wanted them to love Him, 6.5; 1.1.

   Read these verses and decide what they teach about God. Choose one answer:
   1. He is righteous
   2. He is merciful and loving
   3. These verses teach that He is both righteous and merciful.
   4. These verses do not teach that God is righteous or merciful.

   Write in your answer on each line.

   .1 Deuteronomy 1.30 _____

   .2 Deuteronomy 2.26 _____

   .3 Deuteronomy 4.3 _____

   .4 Deuteronomy 7.5 _____

   .5 Deuteronomy 8.14-16 _____

   .6 Deuteronomy 11.6 _____

   .7 Deuteronomy 11.27,28 _____

   .8 Deuteronomy 34.8 _____

   .1 The Lord helped His people and protected them from their enemies; this shows that He *loved* them, 1.30.

   .2 This verse, 2.26, does not refer to God and does not say anything about His love or His righteousness, so 4 is the correct answer.

   .3 The Lord destroyed the wicked sinners so this verse shows that He is *righteous,* 4.3.

   .4 The Lord will punish His own people when they sin; this is because He is and always will be *righteous,* 7.5.

   .5 God cared for Israel as they travelled through the desert, and this shows His great *love* for them, 8.14-16.

   .6 The *righteous* Lord destroyed Dathan and Abiram because they rebelled against Him, 11.6.

   .7 God would bless His people if they obeyed Him and this showed His *love.* He would also curse them if they turned from Him, because He is *righteous* as well as loving, 11.27,28. Answer 3 is correct.

   .8 This verse, 34.8, does not mention God's love or righteousness, so answer 4 is correct.

===

8. The whole Bible speaks of Christ and in the book of Deuteronomy we see several pictures of the Lord. Before we look at these, let us consider what God told Moses to say in 18.15-19. Read these verses, also Acts 3.22, 23, then answer this question: Who is the Prophet like Moses? _____

Peter said that the Lord Jesus Christ is the Prophet like Moses, so Moses' words are a definite prophecy of Christ.

9. There are also pictures of Christ in Deuteronomy. For example, Moses is a picture of Christ as He prays for us. The sacrifices all pointed forward to Christ. These sacrifices had to be perfect, 17.1, and this makes us think of Christ's perfect work.

Some verses remind us of the Lord's work in the past, when He died on the cross; others tell of His present work in heaven as He prays for us. Read each of these verses and decide which part of the Lord's work is suggested, past or present.

1. Chapter 9, verses 26, 27 _____
2. Chapter 12, verse 27 _____
3. Chapter 16, verse 2 _____
4. Chapter 21, verses 3, 4 _____

Some verses speak of the death of an animal as a sacrifice, and these refer to the death of the Lord: 12.27; 16.2; 21.3,4.

Others tell us about Moses praying for the people and we see a picture of Christ in His present work today: 9.26, 27.

10. The Lord Jesus Christ is our Saviour and we will now think about Salvation and what Deuteronomy teaches about it. The Lord Jesus brought grace and truth but the law was given by Moses, John 1.17. There is a great difference between law and grace. Would you say that Deuteronomy is mostly a book of law or grace? _____

The law was given by Moses and in Deuteronomy the law is the most important subject, but we can also see God's grace in many ways.

11. Grace is more wonderful than law, but God's law is very good. Can any man improve God's law by adding something to it, or taking something from it? 4.2. _____

No, Israel were told not to change it. We are also told not to add anything to God's Word or take anything from it, Revelation 22.18,19.

12. What nation had better laws than Israel, 4.8? _____

No nation had a better law than Israel because the one true God had given Israel His law. God's law is perfect, Romans 7.12.

===

6/29 **13.** How did Moses say in short form what God requires, and how can man do what He wants, 10.12,13? _____

_____

God asks men to fear and love Him, to serve Him and to be like Him, 10.12. How can we do this? By keeping all His commands, v.13.

===

14. Did Israel do this? Has any man ever done it? (Romans 3.10 will help you with this question if you are not sure of the answer.) _____

_____

No, all have sinned against God, all Jews and all Gentiles. This is why we all need the grace of God. We cannot do all of God's will, we are sinners, we need a Saviour. Deuteronomy tells us plainly about the law of God, but the New Testament shows us how sinners can be saved; we can be saved by trusting in the Lord Jesus who died for them. [Here is a personal question: Have you ever accepted Christ as your own Saviour? Are you trusting Him right now?]

===

15. Deuteronomy tells us many things about Israel which are also true of us today. For example, Israel was chosen to be a holy nation and we too have been chosen to be holy people for God. Read the verses given in Deuteronomy for both of these things.

    1. Deuteronomy 10.15   Chosen _____

    2. Deuteronomy 7.6; 14.2   Holy _____

Now read Ephesians 1.4 and 1 Peter 1.15,16 and 2.9 and write on the line the correct verses for each of these two things.

_____

Ephesians 1.4 says that God chose us in Christ before the world began, so you should have written this verse after the word *chosen*. The verses in 1 Peter say we are holy or set apart for God and should certainly live holy lives.

===

6/30 **16.** Other verses in Deuteronomy tell us what God wanted Israel to be or to do. Verses in the New Testament show us that God wants us to be or do the same.

    For example, Deuteronomy teaches that:

        1. Israelites should keep themselves separate from the people of the

The Teaching of Deuteronomy

land and should not marry anyone who did not believe in Jehovah, 7.3,4.
2. The people of Israel must judge anyone who tried to persuade them to worship idols, 13.6-11.
3. God had punished them so they would learn to obey Him, 8.5,6.

Read these verses in Deuteronomy, then read others in the New Testament: 1 Corinthians 5.11-13; 2 Corinthians 5.14-18; Hebrews 12.5-11. Write on each line which verses teach the same truth as Deuteronomy does.

1. Deuteronomy 7.3,4   Be separate _____
2. Deuteronomy 13.6-11   Judge sin _____
3. Deuteronomy 8.5,6   God punishes His sons _____

----

1. 2 Corinthians 5.14-18 teaches us to keep ourselves separate from the world and so you should have written these verses after the words *Be separate*.
2. 1 Corinthians 5.11-13 commands us to judge any sin in the church and this is the same truth as in Deuteronomy 13.6-11.
3. Hebrews 12.5-11 shows us that God will punish all His sons, and Deuteronomy 8.5,6 says that God did this to Israel.

===

17. The New Testament also teaches us how we should act as Christians. For example:
    1. We should not be proud of ourselves, but humble, 1 Peter 5.5,6.
    2. We should be ready for the battle and willing to fight for the Lord, Ephesians 6.11-13; 2 Timothy 2.3,4.
    3. We should be very happy because we can have the Lord's own joy in us, John 17.13.

Deuteronomy also teaches these things. Read 7.18; 8.2,3; 12.12. Which of these verses teach the same things as the verses given above?

1 Peter 5.5,6   Humble, not proud _____
Ephesians 6.11-13   Ready to fight _____
John 17.13   Happy in the Lord _____

In Deuteronomy 8.3 we see that the Lord wanted the people of Israel to be humble, so this is the first answer.

In Deuteronomy 7.18 God told them not to be afraid of their enemies; they must be ready to fight against them.

In Deuteronomy 12.12 they should rejoice and be happy before Jehovah.

===

144 Desert Journey

18. The Bible also tells us many things about the future and Deuteronomy mentions a few of them. The most important truth is that God would choose His own King for Israel, Deuteronomy 17.15, and for the whole world. Read this verse and also Revelation 17.14 and then answer this question: Who is God's chosen King? (If you are not sure read also John 1.29.) _____

The Lord Jesus Christ is the Lamb of God and the King of kings.
==

19. God will bless His people when His King comes to rule, but He will be very angry with all men who have rejected His Son. In Deuteronomy 32.22 we can see that God's anger will burn like a fire in Sheol, which is where dead people go. In the New Testament we read about the lake of fire. How long will the lake of fire last according to Revelation 20.10? _____

Forever.
==

So the book of Deuteronomy shows us a great deal about the power and glory of God. The first book in the Bible tells us about God creating all things. The fifth book leads us on to the coming King. God has His plan for all men and it cannot fail. The law was part of that plan and was necessary to show men that they need God's grace. We also have learned many lessons in Numbers and Deuteronomy about God's righteousness and His mercy. These books will help us to become more like God's Son who always did what His Father wanted Him to do.

==

Answers to Questions

Page 19

1. Because Moses counted all the people twice, page 7.
2. From Sinai to Kadesh, page 8.
3. Thirteen months, 1.1.
4. They had a better work for God, page 10.
5. Judea, Reuben, Ephraim and Dan, page 10.
6. God wants His people to live orderly lives in this world, page 10.
7. The tribe of Levi, page 11
8. They paid five shekels each, or 1,365 shekels in all, 3.50.
9. Only the skin of seals or porpoises, page 13.
10. The Kohathites, 4.15.
11. God was angry and a man died, page 14.
12. He must pay it back to the man's nearest relatives, page 14.
13. A family cannot be happy, but God will judge the one who is really guilty, page 15.
14. To show people that he had set himself apart for the Lord, page 16.
15. Samson, who failed because he was weak, page 17.
16. The Lord Jesus Christ, page 18.

Page 31

1. They had to carry the furniture on their shoulders, page 20.
2. Twenty-one, pages 20, 21.
3. a. God values all gifts from His people.
   b. These are the first gifts after the Tabernacle was built.
   c. Everything speaks about Christ. Page 21
4. God will tell us more about Himself if we obey Him, pages 21, 22.
5. Levi, Numbers 8.17, 18.
6. They could serve the Lord in the Tabernacle, but could not carry the burdens, page 22.
7. (1) If he had touched a dead body and was unclean; or (2) if he was on a long journey.
8. To call the people together on feast days and to declare war, page 24.
9. Some of the Kohathites, those who carried the ark, page 26.

10. Moses should have trusted God instead of asking an outsider to be the guide but he showed true faith when he asked God to help Israel, page 26.
11. He sent thousands of quails but the people became very sick, page 28.
12. He chose 70 men to help him, 12.16,17.
13. He was not jealous and would have been glad if they all were prophets, page 28.
14. Perhaps someone else wrote it, but anyway we know it is true, page 29.

Page 45

1. Israel could have entered the land of rest, but they decided to disobey, page 32.
2. No, God had already told them it was good, page 32.
3. They said the men of Canaan were too strong for Israel, page 33.
4. Because Caleb and Joshua wanted them to go on into Canaan, page 34.
5. God forgave the people, but He had to punish them too, page 34.
6. 40 days; 40 years, page 35.
7. The adults could not go into the land but God gave these commands and showed that Israel would enter later on, page 36.
8. By thinking more about Christ, His perfect life and His death, page 37.
9. He knew he was doing wrong and so there was no sacrifice he could bring, page 37.
10. They were not satisfied with the privileges they had as Levites but wanted to be priests like Aaron, page 38.
11. God destroyed Korah and all his followers, then He stopped the disease from spreading when *Aaron* ran among the people. He also caused Aaron's rod to sprout and grow flowers, pages 40,41.
12. The other tribes brought one-tenth of all they owned and gave it to the Levites.
13. God commanded this, 18.12, and it is a picture of the joy of worshipping the Lord, page 43.
14. A clean person would sprinkle some water of purification on him, page 44.
15. A Christian becomes unclean from contact with the world, but washing with the Word of God makes him clean again, page 44.

Page 55

1. He had told him only to speak to the rock and Moses' act spoiled the picture of Christ, page 47.
2. Miriam and Aaron, Moses' sister and brother.
3. The Lord Himself said He would be lifted up and all who believe in Him will have life, John 3.14,15.
4. The princes dug a well and God gave them water, page 50.
5. God encouraged the people of Israel to believe that they would be able to defeat the kings on the west side of Jordan, page 50.
6. Because Israel had destroyed the Amorites, page 51.
7. He offered to pay Balaam if he would curse Israel, page 51.
8. He tried to curse Israel but God would not let him, page 52.
9. Because he was not able to curse Balak's enemy, page 53.
10. It tells us about the way of Balaam, the error of Balaam, and the teaching of Balaam, page 53.
11. He told Balak to send women who could lead the Israelites into sin, page 53.
12. A terrible disease spread among the people and 24,000 died, page 54.

Page 68

1. No, there were about 2,000 less than before, pages 56,57.
2. They had no brothers, so they asked if they could own their father's property after he died, page 58.
3. The Lord did, page 58.
4. 2, 4, 7 - page 59.
5. The death of our Lord Jesus Christ, page 60.
6. His wife was under his authority, but he had to cancel her promise right away or else she would have to do what she had said, pages 60,61.
7. Because Midian had lead many men of Israel into sin and would have done the same again, page 61.
8. By fire and water, page 62.
9. Because they had a lot of cattle and the land east of Jordan was good for cattle, page 63.
10. God had said that Moses should throw lots and He would show where each tribe should live, page 63.

148 *Desert Journey*

11. The names of many places where Israel stopped on their journey through the desert, pages 64, 65.
12. On the edges of the land of Canaan, page 65.
13. So a man could run in and be safe if he killed someone by accident, page 66.
14. So their land would not be owned by a man in some other tribe, page 67.

Page 88

1. Israel could have been in the land of Canaan 38 years earlier if they had obeyed God, page 82.
2. Seventy. Over 60,000 were chosen before, but Moses had not asked God about this, page 83.
3. Fifty-eight, page 84.
4. Ammon, page 85.
5. The Amorites, Bashan, page 85.
6. Because Moses had sinned, page 86.
7. God gave him this great gift.
8. None of them; they must worship God only and they could not make an image of Him because they had never seen Him, page 87.
9. He delivered them from Egypt, spoke to them from the fire and drove out great nations from before them, page 87.
10. We have been justified by the blood of Christ, set apart by the Holy Spirit, and blessed with all blessings, pages 87, 88.
11. Joshua later named three other cities west of Jordan, page 88.

Page 100

1. In Exodus 20, because God rested after creating the earth; in Deuteronomy 5, because God redeemed Israel from Egypt, page 89.
2. No, they were afraid God might come and destroy them, and they thought that they would be able to keep His commands, page 90.
3. The Lord Jesus said the first commandment was the greatest, page 91.
4. Only those who know Him, page 91.

Answers 149

5. Deuteronomy 6.13,16; 8.3, page 91.
6. Not because they were the largest nation but because He loved them and had promised Abraham, Isaac, and Jacob that He would bless their descendants, page 93.
7. Not with large families or lots of money, but with spiritual blessings, joy, peace and victory over sin, page 93.
8. So they would learn that they needed something more than natural food. They must live by every word of God, page 94.
9. Be careful because Satan will tempt us if we get proud, page 95.
10. Because they were very wicked and God had promised the land to Israel, page 95.
11. They rebelled against God at Mount Sinai, Taberah, Massah, Kibroth Hattaavah, and Kadesh Barnea, page 96.
12. The wood reminds us He is a Man and the gold reminds us He is God. The law was placed inside the Ark and the Lord Jesus always obeyed His Father's law from the heart, page 97.
13. It means to cut off the flesh or the old nature and act as though it were dead, page 98.
14. The covenant of law was conditional but the covenant of grace was unconditional, page 99.

Page 111

1. God did not want them to worship the idols of the people who lived in the land before Israel, page 101.
2. Anywhere, but they had to bring their sacrifices to the central place, and could not eat the tenth part of what they got because it belonged to the Lord, page 102.
3. We know he is a false prophet if he teaches us to worship idols or follow some other religion, page 102.
4. Each foot was divided into two parts and clean animals chew their food again after swallowing it, page 103.
5. They gave most of it to the Levites, page 104.
6. He didn't have to pay because it was the year of release, page 105.
7. Because the slave chose to stay with his master and did not want to be free and go away, page 105.
8. Three times a year, for the Feast of Unleavened Bread, the Feast of Weeks, and the Feast of Tabernacles, page 107.
9. The sacrifice was a picture of Christ and He is the perfect One, page 108.

10. No, only the King whom God would choose, page 108.
11. God has commanded us to keep away from spirits because they would lead us into sin, page 109.
12. The Lord Jesus Christ is God's Prophet who told us what God wants us to do, page 110.

Page 112

1. The judges would do to him what he wanted them to do to the other person, page 113.
2. All who were afraid and all who were thinking about other things, a new house, a new vineyard, or a new wife, page 114.
3. The Lord would not hold them guilty, if the elders killed a young cow and declared that they did not know who killed the man, page 115.
4. He feels like a human father who has to punish his son because he would not obey, page 115.
5. We should not try to mix the things of the Lord and the things of the world, page 116.
6. The girl did not have to die if she was caught committing sin in the country because no one could hear her cry for help, page 117.
7. God's grace proved to be greater than His law, page 117.
8. Paul knew that Philemon was a Christian and Paul asked him to be kind to Onesimus, page 118.
9. Only if the other person has committed adultery, page 119.
10. Israel should remember that they had been slaves in Egypt and God had delivered them, page 120.
11. We should be righteous and fair to all men and kind to one another, page 121.
12. Deuteronomy shows us the spiritual meaning of many of the laws, and it is more closely connected with the New Testament, page 122.

Page 137

1. The law can only bring a curse because men do not obey everything, page 125.
2. The law could only curse but the sacrifice on the altar pointed forward to Christ who accepted the curse for us, page 124.

Answers 151

3. Because God knew the people would break His commands, page 126.
4. 2 Kings and 2 Chronicles, page 126.
5. Yes, even those who broke the law were still under God's covenant, page 128.
6. They did not have to go anywhere. It was very near them and Moses himself was still with them, page 129.
7. He lived 40 years in Egypt, 40 years in the desert looking after sheep, and 40 years leading the nation of Israel, page 130.
8. Psalm 90 and perhaps Psalms 91, page 131. Also remember the song of victory in Exodus 15.
9. These are two different names for Israel, page 131.
10. Both sinned at Kadesh-barnea, page 132.
11. Moses and Aaron stood against the rest of the people at Massah and Meribah. Phinehas punished a man for openly sinning against God, pages 133, 134.
12. Twelve, if you count Ephraim and Manasseh, verse 17, and Zebulun and Issachar, verse 18.
13. In John 1.18 the Son is always near the Father and in Acts 7.55,56 He is at God's right hand, page 136.
14. Moses wrote most of Deuteronomy but someone else may have written the last chapter. We can be sure it is true and a part of God's Word, page 136.